NARCISSISTIC FATHER

Discover how to Identify Narcissistic Abuse, Healing Your Wounds, Feeling Better and Having a New Relationship with Your Father

Gwen Evans

DEDICATION

This book is dedicated all those who have survived or are trying to do their best to encounter a narcissistic father but still believe in good things and want to participate in the betterment of world through their positivity.

CONTENTS

PREFACE

<u>Story of Echo and Narcissus</u>
Echo a beautiful nymph, who was very fond of hills and mountains was one of the favourite of goddess Diana. Echo had only one weakness though, that she couldn't live without chattering and talking.

One day Juno got angry with Echo and she passed a sentence upon her whereby Echo lost her power to speak; however, she could only have the last word of her speech, but no power to speak her first words and she was also banished to live among the tall mountains where loneliness was her only partner till the day she saw Narcissus, the most beautiful god who was pursuing the chase high up in the mountains. Echo immediately fell in love with him. she longed to say those sweet words of love to him but all she could made out of her mouth was hollow sound of the last words spurted from her mouth.

One day Narcissus shouted aloud, "Who's here?"

"Here." Echo replied.

Narcissus looked around, but couldn't see no one.

The maid tried to answer with all her heart but it was all in vain. Narcissus left her, and the heartbroken nymph hid herself in deeper caves and among mountain cliffs. Her form faded with grief, till at last all her flesh shrank away. Her bones were changed into rocks and there was nothing left of her but her voice.

There was a clear fountain, with water like silver, where Narcissus went to drink some water, he stooped down to drink water but at the very instant, he saw his own image in the water; he thought it was some beautiful water-spirit living in the fountain. He stood gazing with admiration at those bright eyes, those locks curled like the locks of Bacchus or Apollo, the rounded cheeks, the ivory neck, the parted lips, and the glow of health and exercise over all. He fell in love with himself. He brought his lips near to take a kiss; he plunged his arms in to embrace the beloved object. It fled at the touch, but returned again after a moment and renewed the fascination.

He could not tear himself away; he lost all thought of food or rest, while he hovered over the brink of the fountain gazing upon his own image.

His tears fell into the water and disturbed the image. As he saw it depart, he exclaimed, "Stay, I entreat you! Let me at least gaze upon you, if I may not touch you." With this, and much more of the same kind, he cherished the flame that consumed him, so that by degrees he lost his color, his vigor, and the beauty which formerly had so charmed the nymph Echo.

She kept near him, however, and when he exclaimed, "Alas! alas!" she answered him with the same words. He pinned away and died; and when his shade passed the Stygian river, it leaned over the boat to catch a look of itself in the waters. The nymphs mourned for him, especially the water-nymphs; and when they smote their breasts Echo smote hers also. They prepared a funeral pile and would have burned the body, but it was nowhere to be found; but in its place a flower, purple within, and surrounded with white leaves, which bears the name and preserves the memory of Narcissus.

Thanks

WHAT IS NARCISSISM

Narcissism can be defined as the quest for satisfaction from vanity or egoism centered on self-perfectionist ideas. In other words, the term is commonly used to define anyone with somehow flattered and exaggerated sense of self-worth. The idea further extends to self-flattery, arrogance and extensive self-pride which might demean others for their very existence. The term narcissism originated from old Greek mythology about a young god 'Narcissus' who falls madly in love with his own image, reflected in a pool. Now Narcissism is more commonly viewed as personality disorder which is described in psychoanalytic theory as a mental disorder related to neurosis. The term is given the specific name as "Narcissistic Personality Disorder (NPD)'.

Not only this, Narcissism is also viewed as a social disorder. It is also seen as part of trio of 'Dark Personality Traits' i.e. Narcissism, Machiavellianism and psychopathy.

A personality disorder is the type of psychological ailment which affects a person's thinking, his behavior and ultimately his relations with others. This leads to various defects in one's personality which leads to pathological and sometimes abusing (both to others and self) personality traits.

However, one should not mix the narcissism with healthy self-love, or egocentrism or egoism. They aren't the same.

What is 'Narcissism a Personality Disorder' (NPD)

According to a latest study, everyone, at some stage of his or her life, has some level of narcissistic tendencies. 'Primary Narcissism' which is also described as a form of healthy self-love might not fall in the category of narcissistic disorder, until the time when it starts to affect a person's ability to engage in various relationships with others in a demeaning way.

People who are suffering from NPD usually have the following symptoms:

I. *Demonstration of extreme confidence*
II. *Craving attention*
III. *Little to no empathy for others.*
IV. *low self-esteem under the mask of boasted confidence*
V. *Sadness.*
VI. *Feeling of inadequacy.*
VII. *requiring constant validation from others*
VIII. *inability to form lasting relationships.*
IX. *persistent pathological behavioral patterns.*
X. *General distress*
XI. *Considering oneself very important*
XII. *Non-acceptance of any kind of criticism.*
XIII. *Self-aware (excessive) of their own success & achievements and stressing others to value them for that.*

XIV.   *Having strong need to be admired*
XV.   *Behaving in an arrogant manner that is perceived as conceited, boastful, or pretentious*
XVI.   *seeking relationships only with same level or superior people*
XVII.   *seeking for monopoly in conversations*
XVIII.   *Looking down on people*
XIX.   *Shamelessly Taking advantage*
XX.   *Enviousness about other people's achievements*
XXI.   *Reacting contempt exert superiority.*
XXII.   *Difficulty in handling change*
XXIII.   *Secret feelings of shame, humiliation, insecurity & vulnerability.*

A person diagnosed with narcissism will usually show six to seven symptoms, as described above, which may vary from person to person. At present around 9.4 % of people around the globe have NPD and the disorder is less common in women than men who have higher percentage of NPD than woman.

Moreover, younger people have higher percentage of NPD, and the people who are divorced, widowed, never married or separated. The study also shows that NPD decreases with age. However, the alarming situation is that this personality disorder is overall increasing in great extents in modern Western societies where it is even named as "narcissism epidemic." Research has also found "high co-occurrence" of NPD with anxiety, drug abuse and low self-esteem in people.

Causes of Narcissism

No one really knows what causes this disorder, yet. It usually starts at teenage and the main factors behind this disorder are some kind of complexes rooted in bad or deprived childhood.

The factors which are most commonly considered as the causes of narcissism are the following:

a. **Environment** — bad parent-child relationships. It can either be the excessive praising or excessive admonishing/criticism; both equally play their role in developing complexes and personality disorders.

b. **Inheritance**

c. **Neurobiology** — this is related to 'Coaching & Training' which affects the relationships between behaviors and neurological reactions associated with the particular process.

Narcissism is more frequently observed in men as compared to women. Children can also exhibit narcissistic tendencies but it may not be taken as narcissism as psychology of child is more biased towards self-centeredness which fades away with growing age and the individual leaves off the narcissistic behavior later in life.

Effects of Narcissism

The effects of Narcissistic Personality Disorder vary from depression, anxiety, drug abuse to self, suicidal behavior and thinking patterns leading to physical health problems.

Narcissistic men are also found with an increased amount of cortisol in their blood. Cortisol is a stress hormone and its higher levels can lead to serious health issues related to elevated blood pressure and other diseases of heart.

Who is narcissist?

Narcissist is any individual who suffers from NPD.

a.   Complications & Risk Factors
b.   Complications of NPD can include:
c.   Depression
d.   Anxiety
e.   Relationship disasters
f.   Drugs misuse
g.   Problems at Job place or at school level
h.   Physical health problems
i.   Suicidal behavior

The exact cause of NPD is still unknown, so, it is very difficult to make precautionary measures as there is no properly designed way to prevent this particular personality disorder. However, if measures are taken with proper management and care, there is still a lot of hope that the person suffering from NPD can be saved from the horrific outcomes. The most important thing is to initiate the treatment as soon as you have detected the disorder. The second most important thing is to learn to communicate in order to cope with emotional distress. Seeking guidance from therapists is also very important and helpful. Meditation has been found useful in diverting your inner thoughts and focusing them to on the positive perspective of life.

How to measure Narcissism

The Narcissistic Personality Inventory (NPI) is a type of questionnaire, designed by Robert Raskin and Calvin S. Hall (1979), which is most commonly used to measure NPD. The scores range from 0-40. The higher the score, higher the level of NPD in a person.

***

1.1. A BRIEF HISTORY OF NARCISSISM

The term 'narcissism' originated from the Roman mythology about Narcissus and Echo, created by a Roman poet, 'Ovid' This myth revolves around Narcissus, a young and very charming god and a young nymph named Echo; a pretty maiden who was cursed to speak only the last words spoken by others. She is banished to live among mountains where one day, she sees Narcissus drinking water from one of the waterfalls and immediately falls in love with him. Narcissus sees his own reflection in water (which he has never seen before) and immediately falls in love with his own self as he has never seen someone so beautiful before. Echo tries to talk to Narcissus but fails every time as she can only repeat the last words spoken by others. Narcissus goes to the pool every day and falls more in love with the reflection he sees in water (not knowing its him). Echo dies in the mountains while Narcissus remains so absorbed in trying to persuade his own reflection to love him back. Finding that the reflection won't love him back, his heart breaks and he dies in grief, his eyes still looking at his own reflection and his fingers touching the surface of water where his reflection showed up. The term Narcissism is currently applied to the personality disorder leading to excessive self-love to the extent of arrogance and disrespect for others with no empathy.

The above-mentioned myth depicts the complex

as well as rich history of Narcissism in literature. This myth is the basis to understand the clinical psychoanalysis of NPD, which begins with an abnormal self-focused personality. The term Narcissus was first used by a psychologist named Havelock Ellis in 1898 who used the term "Narcissus-like", clinically, to describe "auto-eroticism in one of his patients. Gradually, the concept of narcissism began to be understood as some kind of personality deformation. It was also given the name "God-complex" because the people suffering from this disorder subconsciously had a behavioral pattern which was a combination of traits like loneliness, inaccessibility, overconfidence, auto-eroticism, excessive self-admiration and extravagant need of uniqueness (that nobody is like them or should be) They also had strong fantasies of them being the omnipotent ones (ruling the world along). This description closely describes the current concept of Narcissistic Personality Disorder.

In 1933, Freud published his essay On Narcissism which was a deeply researched writing from early developmental perspective. He described narcissism as normal growing trait in the healthy children. Freud theorized that children go through a short period of primary narcissism. During this period, they exhibit egocentric attitude where they are quite negative on taking the perspective of others. Freud considered the turn from primary narcissism towards normal personality during the growth as a normal and healthy symbol of growth and development. Freud theory further elaborates the events which might lead a person to develop 'secondary narcissism'. He calls the energy behind love as 'libidinal energy' and theorizes that every individual has a limited energy for love which he invests in other individuals or on himself. Thus, when a person is departing from primary narcissism to sharing their libidinal energy (Love), their primary narcissism is automatically lowered during the healthy reciprocal relationship in which both individuals share equal energy with each other and no problems are created. The primary narcissism leaves the personality for good and everything goes fine. However, the problem arises when the other person (we can call the other person as 'love object) is unwilling or somehow unable to return the love, the person objectifying retreats to a very unhealthy state of mind or simply next state of narcissism, which is called 'secondary narcissism', The person suffering from secondary narcissism adopts a kind of compensatory mechanism in which he tries to gratify himself to compensate the love he is being denied.

Freud further described the narcissistic personality disorder with traits of excessive self-preservation, strong sense of independency, aggressiveness, non-intimidated and somehow highly extrovert. He described the persons with NPD unable commit in relationships. Surprisingly, these people attracted a lot of attention and admiration. They showed high interest in taking up leadership roles.

In 1933, a psychoanalyst 'Wilhelm Reich' described narcissists as a person who possesses a sense of high superiority, arrogance and resenting of subordination. He also described them as provocative and sadistic in relationships. He also observed aggressiveness in narcissists when they were ego-threatened. He wrote in his description:

In the event that their vanity is outraged, they respond with cold contempt, stamped bad mood, or downright aggression.

Reich's also viewed that NPD was more common in men than in women. He was also the one who concluded that outcomes of narcissism might not come out necessarily worst or negative. According to him, the outcomes depended on the intentions of the person and the social context. He described:

Regardless of whether such a sort will turn his vitality to dynamic undertakings or wrongdoing on a huge scale depends, most importantly, upon the conceivable outcomes which the social atmosphere and circumstance accommodate his character to utilize his energies in a sublimated structure.

***

1.3 Specific Behavioral Signs of Narcissism

The specific behavioral traits and signs of a Narcissist have already been described briefly in section 1.1, however, this section discusses the signs and traits in detail as below:

1.Strong Sense of Superiority (entitlement)

Superiority with a strong sense of self admiration is the basic approach of a narcissist. The narcissist usually divides the world in good/bad, right/wrong and fair/unfair views of his own perspectives (rather than being rational) and then acts to support his own views only as if they were the ultimate truths. A narcissist has usually made some kind of hierarchal pattern in his brains where he sits on top and everybody else comes later. Grandiosity becomes a definite characteristic of narcissistic person as the idea of unrealistic sense of superiority roots deep down in his subconscious, causing them to believe that they are the most "uncommon" ones and nobody is sufficiently extraordinary to match to them. They think themselves as the ones who deserve only the best; thus, rejecting anything or anybody which they might think is of average value or is ordinary. Hence, they don't like to be associated with people below their rank or social status. Narcissists also tend to exaggerate about their achievements, winnings and talents. At work, even if they do minimum, they would always exaggerate about how much they have contributed towards a particular task and its successful disposal.   They also tend to live in a fantasy where they are the ultimate stars with unlimited success, brilliance, power and an ideal love. Their fantasies make them feel in control and protect them from their inner hollowness and self-pitying shame, so they would reject or deny any facts or opinions that might contradict with their inner fantasies. In fact, they show extreme defensiveness and rage towards anything that might be a threat to burst their fantasy bubble. They are in constant denial of reality which also affect the people and relationships around them.

2. A need for admiration and constant validation

A narcissist constantly requires and needs admiration. His need is like a rubber tire that gradually loses its rigidity and thus requires a steady input of admiration, applause and validation in an attempt to keep the tire inflated. The don't comply on occasional compliments as they're never enough. So, they tend to surround themselves with such individuals who cater to their obsession for constant validation. The relationship of a narcissist with such individuals is again very selfish as it is entirely based on the effort put up by the admirer. Once there is some kind of gap or interruption in admirer's praise and attention, he becomes the betrayer to the narcissist.

Narcissists also tend to be the most competent one with excessive control on each and every situation and everyone. At some occasion, the excessive 'being the best' need of narcissist takes turns in 'being the worst' at everything. Which means they feel superior by being the most wrong. This is an interesting phenomenon which also helps a narcissist receive concerns which soothes their senses and they take it as a compensation by hurting you passively.

Another essential narcissist's trait is their hunger for attention. Validation only counts only if it comes at the expense of other people's fair emotions. Still, their thirst for admiration and validation doesn't end. Another very negative aspect of a narcissist personally is their inability to appreciate love. It's because inside they don't believe anyone can actually love them. Behind the curtain of self-absorbed bragging arrogance, a narcissist is extremely fearful and insecure.

3. Perfectionism

You can recognize a narcissist through their very significant requirement for everything to be 'Perfect'. They expect everything to happen as they imagine it. This is a painfully incomprehensible demand on their end, which ends in bringing disappointment and hopeless to the narcissist. a great part of the time. Their requirement for perfection drives the narcissist to whine and be continually disappointed.

4. Great need for control

Grabbing hold of everything and bringing them under control is original narcissistic attitude. They are persistently disillusioned with the imperfections life brings, so they desire to control every aspect of life so that they could shape it according to their own sweet will (but that's quite impossible to control life and its various aspects, so again they end up being depressed and aggressive towards life). They demand to be in charge of every situation, with their main priorities set about what each "character" in their control should say or do.   They don't have any clue what's in store next because they have strong tendency to expect only their desired outcomes. They demand that you state and do precisely what they have as a main priority so they can arrive at their ideal decision. You are merely a character in a stage drama designed by them; rather than being some real individual with his own emotions and thoughts.

5. Accusation

Despite the fact that narcissists need to be in charge, they never want to be answerable for the outcomes—except if, obviously, everything goes precisely their way and their ideal outcome happens. At the point when things don't go as indicated by their arrangement or they feel censured or not exactly great, the narcissist puts all the fault and obligation on others.

6. No respect for healthy boundaries

Narcissist people always try to cross other people's boundaries and this habit is usually incorporated in them as their norm conduct. Narcissists can't see that their freedom ends when other person's boundaries begin. They are only OK with the fact that everything is their personal belonging, so they don't actually respect other people's boundaries.

7. Utmost absence of empathy for others

Narcissists don't feel empathy towards others. Sometimes, this absence of sympathy makes them look vulnerable and ashamed but according to study, narcissists usually consider it fine if someone is suffering because it is in their system that they suffered from something too, so now its other person's turn to suffer the same or equivalent.

This absence of compassion makes genuine connections and passionate association with narcissists troublesome or inconceivable. They simply don't see what any other individual is feeling.

8. Everything is an enemy or threat

Narcissists often misread inconspicuous expressions as threat and try to make a big fuss out of everything. Due to this reason, narcissists often take joking as personal attack and respond with rage or aggressiveness. They can't differentiate between sarcasm and real compliments.

9. Lack of Rationalism

As the narcissist people are only aware of their own thoughts and feelings, they can rationally think of whatever is happening around them. So, no matter how one tries to use logic and reason with them-to make them understand the wrongdoings which might be (emotionally) hurting others-they always end up going their own set ways which are totally based on their own emotions. This is because narcissists take most of their decisions by emotionally judging the situation as per their own set of believes.

10. Lack of Attachment

The narcissist's character is divided into their own version of good and bad. As they don't want anybody to shake their belief, they seldom get genuinely attached with anybody.

11. Fear of rejection

The narcissist's whole life is persuaded by some kind of dark, deep rooted fear. They're continually scared of being rejected, disparaged and dismissed.

If you are in a relationship with the narcissist, you will feel that the closer your relationship turns into, the less they will confide in you.

This is because they fear if they become too attached, they will become more vulnerable and their imperfections will be exposed which will get them rejections, which they fear the most. So, they close in their shells and even abandon you because of their own fears.

12. Depression & Anxiety

Narcissists feels depressed and anxious most of the times and the worst scenario is when they try to project their own depression into those who are their close relatives and loved ones. In this way, a Narcissist can transmit their own anxiety to their loved ones so that they may not feel it themselves. This in turn make them feel superior.

14. Protecting their vulnerability

Narcissists can't truly love someone so they always are emotionally needy. Not only this, whenever they are in a relationship, and if the relationship becomes a threat to their vulnerability, they are often the ones who overlap relationships so that someone else is also available who might night attack on their vulnerability and they can switch whenever they want.

15. An inability to work as a team

Narcissists are unable to develop cooperative behaviors which require real understanding of other people's feelings, so it is usually very difficult for them to work in team.

16. Exploits others without guilt or shame

Narcissists lack empathy, so they always use other people to serve their own needs. When it comes to taking advantage of others, they are also the ones who are in front lines and yet they don't feel any remorse or guilt for this malicious interpersonal exploitation.

17. Frequently demeans, intimidates, bullies, or belittles others

Narcissists feel undermined when they see other to have something they need. They're likewise threatened by individuals who don't know them or who challenge them in any capacity. The best way to kill the threat for a narcissist is to prop up their own drooping sense of self is to put those individuals down. They may do it in a pompous manner so as to exhibit how little the other individual is to them. Bullying is a narcissists active tool to attack those they feel threatened from.

18. Maintaining a false-charm personality

Narcissists can be extremely attractive and charming. Their sense to detect and adopt the charms is highly elevated so that they can charm others with their fake personality. Other people sometimes feel very pulled in to their evident certainty and confidence.

19. Highly aggressive to criticism.

Narcissists do not (at all) accept criticism. It is like some atomic bomb attack on their shallow, weaker inner selves. They only want other to appreciate them even if they are wrong. They would simply become your enemies if you criticize them.

20. Low Self-esteem

Narcissists usually have very low self-respect. They don't consider themselves worthy enough to be loved or respected. So, if even they achieve and gain huge respect from others, their image of their own self is always deteriorated in their own eyes.

The brief traits of people who are suffering from NPD have been laid down as below:

I. *Demonstration of extreme confidence*
II. *Craving attention*
III. *Little to no empathy for others.*
IV. *low self-esteem under the mask of boasted*

	confidence
V.	*Sadness.*
VI.	*Feeling of inadequacy.*
VII.	*requiring constant validation from others*
VIII.	*inability to form lasting relationships.*
IX.	*persistent pathological behavioral patterns.*
X.	*General distress*
XI.	*Considering oneself very important*
XII.	*Non-acceptance of any kind of criticism.*
XIII.	*Self-aware (excessive) of their own success & achievements and stressing others to value them for that.*
XIV.	*Having strong need to be admired*
XV.	*Behaving in an arrogant manner that is perceived as conceited, boastful, or pretentious*
XVI.	*seeking relationships only with same level or superior people*
XVII.	*seeking for monopoly in conversations*
XVIII.	*Looking down on people*
XIX.	*Shamelessly Taking advantage*
XX.	*Enviousness about other people's achievements*
XXI.	*Reacting contempt exert superiority.*
XXII.	*Difficulty in handling change*
XXIII.	*Secret feelings of shame, humiliation, insecurity & vulnerability.*

***

1.3 Types of Narcissism

Narcissism has become a vast subject which has various types. The various types of Narcissism are being discussed as below:

Acquired situational narcissism

Acquired situational narcissism (ASN) is the type of narcissism that usually develops at the stage of late adulthood and is caused by excessive fame, wealth or other things that come with stardom. Media, Fans and society plays an important role in imparting this type of narcissism into a person. The person who suffers from ASN usually shows erratic behavior, unstable relationships, and drug abuse and erratic behavior.

Codependency

Codependency is a type of narcissism where a person behaves in exceedingly passive ways that affects the relationships adversely. This is also called as "co-narcissism"

Group Narcissism (Racial Narcissism)

It is a type of narcissism where an individual has an expanded self-esteem of their own group where the individual is also part of the group and involved. While the exemplary meaning of narcissism centers around the individual, Group narcissism states that one can have a comparative too much high opinion of his/her own group (kind), and as a result the whole group acts as a narcissistic entity. Collective narcissism is also related to ethnocentrism; however, these terms stand separate when it comes to actual meaning of each.

Conversational narcissism

Conversational narcissism is when a person is in continuous competition with others to be the center of attention among the others and the tactic used in conversational narcissism is 'persuasiveness'. In social circumstances, a conversational narcissist will in general cow the discussion away from others and toward themselves. It happens in casual discussions among companions, family and colleagues. The conversation is usually well mannered, full of etiquettes and disciplines which make this type of narcissism as one of the most commonly faced and practiced in regular life.

Cultural narcissism

In Cultural Narcissism, every relationship and activity are built and developed by a cultural narcissist to acquire as much wealth as possible. The decadent need to reach that status and then centralizing every movement and relation around those who will help such narcissist to get those symbols of wealth slowly turns the person into a selfish and hollow individual where none of his relationship are real. Slowly, the whole culture starts revolving around these norms and liberalism as well as progressivism just exists to the extent that they only serve a small society of consumers (customers). As a result, religion, art, and sex lose their liberty. Resultantly, a wave of constant competition among individual takes over and an environment develops where there are no allies and the society are filled with many non-transparent factors. The fears of acquisitions of social status hold strongly to the extent that competition and defensiveness turns into a lifestyle. Any genuine feeling of real society is crushed and replaced with virtual counterparts that in a non-succeeding manner, try to create a sense of society.

Dangerous narcissism

Dangerous narcissism is defined as the steady exhibition of various intense and serious attributes of one's personality typically connected with imparting destruction to other things or even individuals if a destructive narcissist is threatened by someone else and feels vulnerable.

Malignant narcissism

Dangerous narcissism is a disorder which is actually a combination of two disorders i.e. Narcissistic Personality Disorder (NPD), the Antisocial Personality Disorder (APD) The Malignant narcissist experiences elevated levels of mental satisfaction (also called psychological gratification) from achievements over time which only makes this disorder worsened because such type of narcissists turns out to be progressively engaged with this psychological gratification; resultantly, he develops paranoia, schizophrenia and other antisocial disorders. This is considered as the most severe form of narcissism in terms of destruction of personality.

Medical narcissism

Therapeutic narcissism is defined as the habit of 'Health Professionals' to assert their competence in order to preserve their 'self-esteem' to the extent which will even compromise the health of their patients. Often, very capable and even extraordinary talented professional can fall into the trap of Medical Narcissism leading to medical errors and their consequent legal effects.

Workplace Narcissism

Workplace Narcissism is identified with certain kinds of conduct in the work environment. For instance, making other colleagues look low in front of those who are superior, leg-pulling, or even getting someone fired because of professional jealousy fall in the category of workplace narcissism.

Sexual narcissism

Sexual narcissism has been portrayed as an egocentric example of sexual conduct that includes an inflated feeling of sexual capacity and privilege. Sexual narcissism is also when one considers himself as the ultimate superb lover with the perfect preoccupation one's own erotic desires. Sexual narcissism is a dysfunction of intimacy in which sexual adventures are sought after, generally in the form of extramarital affairs, to overcompensate for low confidence and a general inability to encounter genuine intimacy.

Narcissistic Parents

Narcissistic parents are characterized by such type of parents who demand certain type of conduct and behavior from their kids since they see their children as augmentations of themselves, so the child must represent them to the world in a way that may satisfy their own 'emotional needs'. Narcissistic parenting results in tangled, estranged and complex relationships with the children which is accompanied with the feeling of hatred, resentment, emotional gap, self-destructive (even suicidal feelings) in the children. This type of narcissism is the result of many other types of narcissisms as parents would purposefully make a circumstance to gather Narcissistic stockpile so it can also be termed as the 'Root of all other types of Narcissism'

Narcissistic Leadership
Narcissistic leadership or Narcissistic administration is often taken as both healthy as well as destructive in the context that one type can readily convert into other and vice versa.

Types of Narcissists

The toxic narcissist
This type of narcissist persistently causes drama and misery in other people's lives. The drama often leads to pain and destruction to others.

How to identify a Toxic Narcissist?
If you have someone in your life who constantly requires your attention and time and if you can't give

it to them due to some reason, they don't respond well. You might be dealing with someone who is toxic narcissist.

The psychopathic narcissist

A psychopath is very unstable and aggressive person, who would succumb to violence and may cause physical harm to other with no remorse for such bad behavior.

How to identify a Toxic Narcissist?

Very unstable and aggressive persons

Mostly "Serial killers" in history are considered psychopathic narcissist.

The introvert narcissist

An introvert narcissist is one who doesn't inflict their personality upon others or society but firmly believes in the characteristics of narcissism. That can mean a large group of things, including feeling entitled, continually requiring others to respect them, being distracted with progress, being envious of others, and lacking sympathy.

How to identify a Toxic Narcissist?

This one can be trickier to spot than different kinds of narcissists in light of the fact that the individual isn't constantly evident about their issue.

The exhibitionist narcissist

This type of narcissists tells everybody around them that they are narcissistic. An exhibitionist narcissist deliberately exploits others by taking their advantage and is arrogant and haughty with self-centered tendencies. They always try to be in spotlight and get awkward if spotlight isn't fixed on them.

The bullying narcissist

This type of individual is suffering from tow type of personality disorders; self-absorption and harassing others. Bullying narcissists grow themselves by destroying others. They extract their happiness from the sadness they impart on others.

The seducer narcissist

This is an especially precarious kind of narcissist: They will "cause you to feel incredible about yourself just to 'win' you over as a sexual victory.

Classic Narcissists

These are the typical attention seeking, bragging, arrogant, self-absorbent narcissists who boast about their achievements, anticipate that others should complement them, and feel qualified for extraordinary treatment. They get exhausted when the focal point of the discussion goes to anybody else. They are mostly desperate to feel significant and important than the vast majority around themselves.

Vulnerable Narcissists

This type of Narcissists hates the spotlight. They tend to attach themselves to certain special persons in order to dwell in the shadow of that other special someone. They charm others through their expanded generosity in order to get the attention and adoration. They are harmful to be relied on emotionally.

Malignant Narcissists

Malignant Narcissists are very manipulative and extremely exploitative ones. These narcissists have numerous reserved antisocial attributes that make them look like psychopaths and sociopaths. Their objective is to command and control and to achieve their objective, they don't hesitate to utilize deceit and animosity with associated aggression. They also take pleasure from the suffering of other individuals around them.

1.4 *Narcissistic Gaslighting*

The term "Gaslight" refers to the range of practices, in which a partner attempts to control the other partner by manipulating him/her to accept things which are altogether false and plainly bogus. Present day Gaslighting happens in a relationship in which one of the two partners is self-centered, manipulative, conceited, lacking compassion, and has a personal stake in continually being the right one. This is another aspect of Narcissistic Personality Disorder (NPD) which affects the relationship and the person being 'gas-lightened' adversely. In this disorder, the person who is suffering, wouldn't even mind driving the partner crazy by making him/her doubt the reality of his/her own thoughts and perceptions.

If you are involved with somebody who is suffering from this disorder, you will feel your level of confidence and trust in yourself shaken when you are around your partner. Your level of confusion, suspicion and self-doubt will rise and uncertainty would take place of certainty when it comes to making decisions. You will also find yourself feeling the following emotions quite often when you are with your 'gas lightening partner'

a. *They will attempt to convince you to question the perfection of your senses and the quality of your thoughts.*

b. *They would attempt to persuade you that your belief isn't right at the same time convincing that they are right.*

c. *They would react aggressively (or poorly) if you would refuse to accept their version of truth.*

d. *They would try to keep up the argument even you have dropped the same.*

e. *They would try to bully you if until you admit that they are right and you are totally wrong.*

f. *They would try to twist the facts.*

g. *They would try to show themselves as victims and you would end up being the faulty one.*

h. *They would blame you for their own wrongdoings.*

Reasons for Gaslighting

You might be gaslighted for the following most common reasons:

Deceit (hiding):

Your partner wants to conceal something that they are doing in hiding from you. They will try to persuade you to question any evidence that might be a proof for their wrongdoing or that may cause them to feel embarrassed, or may result in negative consequences. This can be something gentle, yet humiliating, (for example, proof that they have been taking a gander at web pornography).

A typical situation includes you discovering something that riddles you. From the outset you think there must be a straightforward clarification, so you notice this to your partner. Your partner passionately denies anything unusual is going on. The reaction is so lopsided to your inquiry that it makes you increasingly suspicious. You begin to focus on things that you recently disregarded. As the proof that your life partner is lying fires accumulating, you become increasingly stressed. At some point, you defy the person in question with the proof. Your partner denies the entire thing and attempts to persuade you that you are suspicious and envisioning this since you are a shaky or envious individual.

Change:

Your partner wants to change you (or something about you). They need to transform you with the goal that you are nearer to their own idealistic figure. They don't acknowledge you for who you truly are. This can include anything from dressing to perusing you get under knife for changing your looks according to their visualization about you. If you don't agree with them, they would attempt to persuade you that you aren't good enough.

Control:

Your partner wants to control you in an attempt to have more power over your actions. Narcissistic partner often wants to be the influencer who needs to approve and control every action of yours. In their attempt to do so, they won't even hesitate to separate and isolate you from those who are respected and admired by you. Once you have permitted your partner to have control over you, slowly, they would start controlling other aspects of your life you reach at a stage where you become hesitant to make your decisions on your own.

NARCISSISTIC FATHER

***

RECOGNIZING NARCISSISTIC FATHER

"Half the harm that is done in this world is due to people who want to feel important. They don't mean to do harm, but the harm (that they cause) does not interest them. Or they do not see it, or they justify it because they are absorbed in the endless struggle to think well of themselves."

(T.S. Eliot)

A narcissistic parent can be characterized as somebody who potentially participates in a sort of competition and rivalry with the child. Commonly, the narcissistic parent sees the freedom of a kid as a risk, and pressures the child to live in their shadow, with irrational expectations. In a narcissistic child rearing relationship, the kid is never admired or encouraged to be himself or herself.

Various investigations have been led regarding the matter of narcissistic child rearing and its effect on the child. It's critical to differentiate certain parent-driven inclinations from extreme narcissistic parenting is an inescapable inclination to deny the child of his/her natural inclinations. To a Narcissistic parent, the child exists just to serve the narrow-minded needs and maneuvers of the parent.

We are part of a world where families are the first and foremost social experiences that we undergo since the very beginning of our lives. Over the course of our growth, it becomes regular that we take our families for granted. Every family is a scaled down sociological trial, with its own arrangement of unwritten principles, hidden facts, and nuanced standards of conduct. We underestimate our mother and father. We take our siblings for granted. And it's quite natural that we do; until you recently accepted the fact that your dad is narcissistic and unlike other fathers.

Here are a few signs that will help you determine if your father has narcissistic tendencies or is narcissist.

2.1 Recognizing Specific Behavioral Traits of Narcissistic Father

- Look if your dad is 'Self-Centered' who has expanded feeling of pretentiousness that persuaded he was better and simply the best.
- Look if your dad exploits others (especially family members including your mother, siblings, and other relatives) to the point of abusing them for his own benefit.
- Look if your dad demands obligation to his orders from everybody. Does he expect everyone to obey his commands?
- Does your dad allude charm in an attempt to allure everyone around him to feel proud in

being associated with him in one or other way? Does he savor profound respect from others and adores being in the spotlight?

- Look if your dad always needs to be the center of attention.
- Look if your dad exaggerates and boasts about his achievements and his goals and ambitions verged on unreasonable objectives.
- Look if your dad has expanded sense of prestigious self and he often fantasizes his success, brilliance, distinction and grandiosity. (He would regularly overstate his accomplishments, and his achievements)
- Does your dad take criticism well?
- Look if your dad tries to cut off all such people from his life who dare criticized him or tried to hurt him with bitter truth.
- Look if your dad's rage is sometimes unreasonable or unreasonable scary. Does he yell by becoming frantic and holler a ton?
- Look if your dad is detached, unsympathetic and generally aloof. Narcissists can't really feel empathy for others (even if it's their own family); they deliberately invalidate other people's feelings with ignorance and negation. Look if your father has regard for his own feelings only. (he doesn't care if somebody else if hurt except for himself)
- Look if your dad remains around to support his family, financially and emotionally as well. Does he get a great deal of satisfaction outside

the family? Do you feel that other fathers spend a lot of time with their families while your father is mostly away?

- Look if your father is more concerned by what others thought of him, as opposed to how his own children felt about him.
- Look if your dad gives you support and freedom enough to take your own decisions.
- Does your dad want you to look extraordinary to his companions and partners? You are only important to him if you are in a position to be bragged about.
- Look if you feel you couldn't generally get what you actually wanted from him. Look if you feel denied and deprived on a subtle and ignorable level.

If answer to most of the above-mentioned traits in your dad is 'Yes' or most of them are evident, then it means your father is a narcissist and suffering from a Narcissistic Personality Disorder (NPD).

Narcissism might not be as dirty a word as its horrific affects are. Truth be told, narcissistic qualities are generally found in the vast majority of us. Narcissistic Personality Disorder, a dubious yet regularly supportive mark. For the record, our analytic classes are to some degree subjective and come up short on the veracity of harder therapeutic demonstrative names. Character or Personality Disorders assist us in developing our thinking about honest depiction of our whole complex selves.

Sometimes, it's genuinely difficult to differentiate whether an individual is narcissistic or only has a higher sense of self-respect. Narcissism isn't tied in with having high fearlessness or self-confidence; it's an affection for oneself that has transformed into a distraction.

Despite the fact that it's not really deadly, narcissism can turn out to be obsessive to the point that it fulfills the criteria of a faulty or dysfunctional personality as under:

1. having a feeling of privilege
2. lacking compassion
3. wanting to be appreciated
4. being exploitative
5. arrogance
6. envious of others

Another trademark regular of narcissists father is a dismissal for children's personal boundaries (to the extent to believe their children to be their personal belonging/property). A narcissist father will treat his own children, and other people that are close to him, as though they are there to satisfy his needs and desires.

How a Narcissistic Father Can Hurt His Children?

Narcissistic Father regularly harm his kids. He may dismiss personal boundaries of kids, control his kids by retaining love, and a general disrespect to child's wishes and dreams including child's career focuses. Since picture is so essential to narcissists, they may request flawlessness from their kids. The offspring of a narcissist father can, thusly, feel a strain to increase their abilities, looks, and charms. It costs the child in both ways; whether he fulfils dad's wishes and meets the expectation, or he fails to meet the same.

Overall, a narcissistic dad can influence a girl or a boy in a manner as described below:

Narcissistic Father and his effect on his daughter

A girl needs her father's admiration and adoration as it encourages her to be unique and confident. Normal dads give their young ladies that blessing. Every girl has a tender heart which needs love and admiration that must come from her father.

However, daughters of narcissistic dads feel "uncertain and confused" satiated" with regards to getting what they required from their dads. Resultantly, when it comes to dealing with relationships, especially with men (or even women), such girls feel helpless and stressed that they'll be dumped for another person. Restlessly maintaining a strategic distance (avoiding commitment) or Gaslighting he partner would become the two choices of such a girl when she grows up and both choices end up in general loss.

Narcissistic Father and his effect on his Son

As the son of a narcissistic dad, he often feels 'left out' and with no confidence. Such child will always feel a certain emptiness in himself, even if he succeeds, despite everything feel vacant and below average.

Much the same as young ladies should be venerated by their dads to feel approved, young men likewise need their father to have faith in them.

Some other important traits for recognizing Narcissistic Father are discussed below in larger details.

2.2 Marginalization

Some narcissistic fathers are genuinely threatened by their child's capacity, talent, potential and achievement, as it feels to them some sort of challenge that may shatter their hollow castle of superiority. Thus, a narcissistic mother or father may put forth a purposeful attempt to put the kid down, so he or she may remain prevalent. Marginalization includes the following:

- Unnecessary Criticism
- outlandish judgment and reactions,
- unfavorable comparisons with other children
- negation of decisions
- invalidation of positive emotions
- rejection of achievement of child's accomplishments

The purpose of marginalization is to lower the child's confidence and boost one's own self-esteem and worth.

The most common phrase used by a narcissistic father (or parent) towards his child might be "You'll never be good enough."

In an attempt to marginalize the child, such father might fulfil the child monetary needs after mentioning in profound sense that it was a waste of money to spend on him/her.

Some narcissistic fathers anticipate that their youngsters should deal with them for the remainder of their lives. This kind of reliance can be enthusiastic, physical, and additionally budgetary. While there's nothing inalienably amiss with dealing with more seasoned guardians – it's a splendid characteristic – the narcissistic parent ordinarily controls a posterity into making outlandish penances, with little respect for the posterity's own needs and needs.

Some narcissistic fathers may likewise move their grown-up kids into codependency. Similarly, some narcissistic parents are compromised by their posterity's latent capacity, guarantee, and achievement, as they challenge the parent's confidence. Thusly, a narcissistic mother or father may put forth a purposeful attempt to put the child down, so the parent stays prevalent. Instances of this kind of serious underestimation incorporates criticizing, preposterous judgment and reactions, ominous examinations, refutation of inspirational dispositions and feelings, and dismissal of progress and achievements.

Numerous narcissistic parents have an erroneously inflated sense of grandiose self-portrait, with a vain sense about what their identity is and what they do. Frequently, people around the narcissist are not treated as individuals, however just devices of exploitation.

2.3 Superficial Image

Superficial image means a narcissistic parent would always show and boast other about their specialty and uniqueness. They make a special effort to look for attention and blandishment. They may brag about their physical appearance, superior dispositions, their accomplishments, their material possessions, contacts with high ups, background and memberships, and successful children only.

For some narcissistic fathers, public interpersonal communication is where they routinely promote how awesome and begrudge commendable their lives are.

Certain narcissistic fathers are exceptionally inflexible with regards to the normal practices of their children. They direct their children on minor subtleties and can become vexed when there's deviation. Some narcissistic fathers are additionally delicate. Purposes behind disturbance towards a child can change significantly, from the kid's absence of consideration and dutifulness, to saw issues and weaknesses, to being within the sight of the parent at an inappropriate time, and so forth.

One purpose behind the parent's firmness and delicateness is the longing to control the youngster.

The narcissist reacts contrarily and disproportionally when she or he sees that the posterity won't generally be pulled by the strings.

2.4 Superiority

Numerous narcissistic parent's guardians have an inflated sense of ego and self-esteem which is overlapped by a proud sense about what their identity is and what they do. Regularly, people around the narcissist are not treated as individuals, rather just apparatuses to be utilized for some benefit or other. It's quite natural that a few children of a narcissistic parent turn to be the same superficial, arrogant narcissists while others who don't turn the same way are somehow pressurized, both consciously as well as subconsciously, to have the equivalent superiority complex. This feeling of gaudy privilege, is solely founded on shallow, egoistical and material basis, which costs oneself his humanity, goodness and conscience.

A narcissistic father quite often believes that his children will only dwell on his influence, so it's also quite normal that he would become jealous (even envious from inside) if the child shows any trait of freedom and independence.

This becomes serious when an adult child wants to have a healthy romantic relationship in their lives as the narcissistic father takes it as a major threat. The reaction of such parent is extreme criticism, rejection and admonishing the child with manipulative sentiments. Some fathers would go to the extent of harming the lover of their child or manipulating the truth into making the child believe that such partner is not good enough (or is a cheater etc.)

Firmly identified with vainglory, numerous narcissistic guardians love to show others how "unique" they are. They appreciate publically marching what they think about their unrivaled miens, be it material belongings, physical appearance, activities and achievements, foundation and participation, contacts in high places, and additionally trophy life partner and posterity. They make a special effort to look for sense of self boosting consideration and sweet talk.

2.5 Manipulation through Emotional Blackmail

The narcissistic parent seems to make a solicitation, yet it is actually a demand. On the off chance that you state no, set limits, or let them realize you'll hit them up later, they will apply expanded weight and undermine outcomes to attempt to get you to submit to them. If you reject, they may then rebuff you with sulking, detached forceful articulations, a fierceness assault, retaining of something significant, or even the risk of savagery or damage.

A narcissistic parent doesn't think logically. There is frequently no reasonable purpose to their allegations, in light of the fact that their world is resolved exclusively by their intuitive sentiments. They will endeavor to disregard any proof that recommends they are incorrect, leaving you baffled that you can't talk any detect into them. Nonetheless, there are a couple of things they will say that essentially constantly mean they don't have any sensible contentions for why they need you to follow their requests, and are currently attempting to sincerely control you into going along. The most common manipulative statements used by a narcissistic parent might be one of the following:

- *"I gave birth to you."*
- *"Raised you on my own/with little help."*
- *"Try not to be so dissatisfied to the dad who gave you everything."*
- *"You are little disrespectful devil."*
- *"Don't dare talk to me like that. I am not your parent"*
- *"If not for me, you'd be (in a terrible circumstance)."*
- *"I'll give you something just when you do as I state."*

A Narcissistic parent's strongest manipulation tool is shaming the child. They disparage and belittle them. This works for little kids very well as the research has indicated that when somebody feels imperfect and damaged, they will in general be increasingly consistent to the solicitations of others.

2.6 Neglect

In certain circumstances, a narcissistic parent may decide to concentrate fundamentally on her or his self-retaining interests, which to the narcissist are more energizing than a child. These exercises may give the narcissist the incitement, approval, and pomposity she or he hungers for, be it vocation fixation, social colorfulness, or individual undertakings and diversions. The kid is left either to the next parent, or on their own.

Parental inability to understand a child, when choices are accessible, is not quite the same as inability to give when choices are not accessible.

Negligence relies upon how a child and society sees the Fathers' conduct; it isn't the way Fathers accept they are carrying on towards their child.

Neediness and absence of resources are regularly contributing elements and can keep Fathers from addressing their child's needs, however, that's another subject. A narcissistic parent would deliberately neglect the child just to make the child feel helpless so that such a parent can gain more control by providing the controlled help. The conditions and deliberateness must be analyzed before characterizing conduct as careless.

2.7 Unsympathetic and Aloof

One of the most widely recognized indications of a narcissistic dad or mother is the powerlessness to be aware of the youngster's own thoughts and feelings and approve them as genuine and significant. Just what the parent thinks and feels matters.

Kids under this sort of parental impact often feel down at confidence and shaky in their disposition. They end up escaping from their fathers. Some children start to Freeze and substitute their discredited genuine self with a bogus persona, in this manner embracing characteristics of narcissism themselves.

Most fathers need their kids to succeed. However, narcissistic parent sets desires not to support the kid just for the satisfaction of their own narrow-minded needs and dreams.

Rather than bringing up a kid in a healthy manner and supporting his/her dreams, Narcissistic parent tries to turn the child into a negligible expansion of the parent's own set of wishes, with the child's own existence reduced.

2.8 Inflexibility & Control

Certain narcissistic fathers are extremely rigid with their children when it comes to general behavioral patterns. They direct their children on every little thing which becomes vexing after a while. Some narcissistic fathers are very tricky and effortlessly activated so easily triggered by even small things done by their children.

One explanation behind the parent's rigidness and instability is their desire and need to control the kid. The narcissist reacts adversely and disproportionally when the child won't generally be pulled by the strings.

Once the narcissistic parent tries to control the child, he is under the adoration which is opposed to the regular articulation of solid child upbringing. Then again, the retention of affection is utilized as danger.

Since a narcissistic mother or father regularly trusts that the kid will forever stay under the parent's impact, she or he may turn out to be incredibly threatened at any indications of the kid's developing development and freedom. Any apparent demonstration of an independent personality-whether it's picking of favourite subjects at college or getting into some relationship, are affected by a narcissistic parent's unhealthy desire to hold control. Finally, a child's natural instinct for investing energy in one's own needs, are deciphered contrarily to the actuality.

It's quite common that a narcissistic parent would expect his children to take care of him for the rest of his life. This is also a type of control which a narcissistic parent wants to have on the child for a lifelong duration.

This dependency is rooted for emotional, financial as well as physical aspects of life. The narcissistic parent usually manipulates the child/children for sacrificing his/her own dreams so that such a parent can exploit the same for his own benefits.

A narcissistic parent also maneuvers the adult ones into "codependency".

Narcissism doesn't need to be obvious. It can appear in little manners and frequently under the pretense of giving a valiant effort for the children or giving them openings, they were denied of when they were pretty much nothing. For example, it's understandable that some fathers would want to enroll their child in basketball team because they didn't get the chance to play, but they also have to notice if the child even likes basketball. They might bring home shirts in monochromatic colors because that's what they like, but they have to notice what colors the child is attracted to. While they want the child to attend the regular school because it worked for them, think about whether they've asked if it will work for the child as well.

Narcissists have a way of making everything about them—they take up all of the air in the room. Their absolute need for attention and appreciation replaces everyone else's needs. Unchecked, a parent's narcissism eclipses a child's feelings. Narcissistic fathers take their children's every feeling or action personally. These fathers are easily angered when a child does not agree with them or denies them. Fathers with narcissistic inclinations are so touchy to gratefulness and appreciation as fuel that it makes them excessively delicate to criticism. So, children learn to tiptoe around these emotional minefields, trying not to trigger that anger, or worse, have their fathers withdraw love.

Keen children will similarly get on the enthusiastic helplessness of their folks. They will praise their parent or attempt to be an ideal impression of them. They trust that dealing with mother or father will support the parent enough so the individual can inevitably return to dealing with them. With the entirety of that care coordinated at fathers, these kids will probably put some distance between their own feelings and needs.

If they grew up with narcissistic fathers, the inheritance can be shared forward.

To begin with, they need to lament the loss of the parent they never had. Truly lament the way that they didn't get the parent they required, the person who put they and the needs first. Some portion of that requires discharging the dream that the narcissistic parent can change and in the long run give they what they need. They can advance and develop; however, they may never advance enough to meet the most profound needs. In this way, overseeing desires is critical, especially when they see looks at the sound parent, they wish they had, yet in truth those impressions are frequently not maintainable. Permit themselves to feel the sentiments, the resentment and the bitterness. Allow permit the feelings to travel through them.

They are going to need to find limits. At the point when they pick who they need to be, as opposed to what other people needed them to be, they can break free from their narcissistic hold. Endure their uneasiness, regardless of whether they make a ton of commotion.

They are being them. This would be the initial segment of breaking the cycle.

Since a narcissistic mother or father regularly trusts that the child will for all time abide under the parent's impact, she or he may turn out to be amazingly envious at any indications of the kid's developing development and autonomy. Any apparent demonstration of individuation and partition, from picking one's own subject choices, to making companions not affirmed by the parent, to investing energy in one's own needs, are deciphered contrarily by a narcissistic parent. Such a parent doesn't want to lose any bit of control. So, he/she does his best to keep the child entangled in a series of commands and directions, at the same time manipulating and

gaslighting the child with maximum strength.
***

PSYCHOLOGICAL DAMAGES OF HAVING A NARCISSITIC FATHER

What happens to the improvement of our character and personality when we live in the shadow of a narcissistic parent?

Do we develop normally?

Or our personality is specifically affected by the particular behavior we have received from our narcissistic father. If character is nothing but a mirror of our relationships, then of course, having a narcissistic father has its adverse effects which may haunt us for the rest of our lives.

Inconsistently sensitive kids develop the tendencies to sort out their lives around the satisfaction of others, persuaded by the idea that they need to support other people's ideas (at the cost of losing their own). They develop this habit of intently disapproving their own cravings or impulses. For such a such, the best life is when it's totally organized and revolves around the joy & happiness of others. They are convinced that they have to nourish and protect the esteem of other people only, even if it is at the cost of their own esteem. An emotionally afraid child would always end up turning into a grownup who is constantly worried about anything & everything. Such a child would tend to hate any such sentiment or needs of their own which they may think is against the general idea of other people or in any sort, is some burden to other people around him/her.

Following are some of adverse effects due to influence of a narcissistic father on the personality of a child:

3.1 Echoism

"Echoism is the phenomenon where someone tries to (or only can) say or act according to what others may direct him to say or act"

Echoism is a personality disorder which is brought upon the child by a narcissistic parent, especially if the child is very sensitive and delicate in his/her disposition and character.

Echoism is derived from the old roman myth about 'Narcissus' and 'Echo' where 'Echo' was a nymph who fell in love with Narcissus while Narcissus was busy all the time staring at himself only and falling in love with his own reflection.

Narcissistic father often drives the child to develop 'Echoism' by not allowing him/her express inner thoughts and dreams. Resultantly, child finds it normal to occupy as meager space as could be allowed, by thinking that expressing his/her own desires and dreams might be an act of extreme selfishness on their part.

Just Like the nymph 'Echo', the echoists always try to have their very own voice and to be able to express themselves fully but they feel entangles and cages in themselves.

This unreasonable conviction can lead a person to shape associations with 'overwhelming' characters — individuals who take up a ton of the conversational space. Consider it a great "opposites are inclined toward one another" circumstance. Echoists may end up in entirely controlling connections where their needs and emotions are overseen discredited, disgraced, and nullified.

Echoists, just like 'Echo' end up in extremely narcissist relationships where they waste all their energies in trying to make their partner realize how much they love him/her, but just like Narcissus couldn't listen and understand Echo, similarly, echoists end up drained out of all their energy wasted upon their narcissistic partner. Despite how it starts echoism, similar to any quality, endures paying little heed to whom individuals invest their energy with. All things considered, Echoists are frequently attracted to narcissists absolutely in light of the fact that they're so scared of troubling others or appearing to be "destitute". They constantly look for somebody who relishes occupying all the space, as narcissists regularly do, comes as something of a consolation; however, it's a significant expense to pay for a relief from their tensions. At the point when narcissists become injurious, echoists now and then convince themselves worthy of all the abuse they have been enduring on themselves. Despite the fact that nobody deserves to be misused or abused, regardless of whether they remain in a relationship or not — misuse is 100 percent the duty of the abuser — however echoists can soil themselves in damaging connections, since they feel liable for their abuse. This leads to general personality distortion. This effect of a narcissistic father on a child makes the child vulnerable to any exploitation whether it's bullying, taken for granted or left behind by other narcissists around him/her.

As Echoists seem to be the most sensitive people than the majority of us — they feel a great deal of emotions which can mislead them in a great deal — and when that disposition is presented to a parent who disgraces or rebuffs them for having any requirements whatsoever, they may tend to drive themselves towards 'extreme echoism.

Extreme echoists generally have an idea that communicating their needs will cost them love, so they tend to put some distance between their own wants. The biggest problem with the Echoists is that they never feel exceptional and special— and they languish over it. To numerous individuals, this may appear to be astounding. It's obvious from the examination that feeling a little uncommon assists individuals with continuing notwithstanding disappointment, think beyond practical boundaries, and perhaps live more.

Echoists don't know that they are also normal individual who also deserve all the respect, high self-esteem and praising like normal people do. They start considering themselves doormats (with contend emotions about it). They may censure themselves for terrible associations, however they're uniquely headed to abstain from feeling like a weight, so they can blow up if someone starts giving them importance (like wishing them on their birthday). They become the people who never want any special efforts made for them. Some extreme echoists are so worried about turning into a weight that they detach themselves to restrain their communications, turning out to be furiously "counter dependent," pushing all demonstrations of nurturance with "Don't treat me like that; I'll be fine!"

Echoism is essentially the result of narcissistic upbringing of a child which turns the child to feel less important about himself/herself. A narcissistic parent can easily pass on the fear to the child that demanding any special treatment is off limits. A normal child might go through this without being affected at all but when it comes to a sensitive and emotional child, he/she may take it adversely (and personally) so he/she may be become an echoist. Whether the echoism is mild or extreme, it's absolutely the product of narcissistic upbringing of a child which costs him/her later in life.

3.2 Self-Blaming

Narcissistic fathers could possibly be clearly abusive, however they're genuinely indifferent to the emotional pain that their abuse might be causing to the child. Such fathers are excessively distracted with their own interests to even hear the pain of their pain. Sensitive children long for affection. When that affection isn't given to them, they don't go out finding the same from other resources, rather they end up blaming themselves by thinking that they must have done something wrong which makes them not worthy of the affection of their parent. Eventually, they lose all their self-esteem and confidence thinking themselves to be the useless and unwanted ones.

Self-blaming is one of the most harmful types of psychological misuse of ones own self. It intensifies our apparent insufficiencies, genuine or fantasized, and incapacitates us before we can even start to move ahead towards doing something good for our lives. While we are normally guided to spread and benevolence to other people, we regularly fail in first giving it to ourselves.

One factor that essentially adds to our arrangement of self-blaming is the inability to perceive our own worth as humankind. We are, from one perspective, impeccable creatures. Then again, we are particularly people—impeccable in soul, not all that ideal in our flesh. However, instead of holding space or recognizing this standing twofold edged part of the human condition, we regularly abide in the hallucination of our hairsplitting. This type of thinking pattern is essentially the outcome of narcissistic upbringing which causes a person to hold some kind of grudge against his/her own self resulting into self-shaming for little things in life. When a person creates a kind of hallucination into believing that the only way to exist is the perfect sense that the world has laid around himself, he starts trying to fit into the picture but a narcissistic parent can make a person believe that he would never be good enough to meet that criteria; that's where the vicious cycle of self-blaming starts.

When it is possible that we or the world we make around us doesn't meet this fanciful perfect, we become regularly adept to take on flaw and a resultant obligation that isn't even our responsibility. Our inability to perceive the parity of duty in some random circumstance drives us into the snare of mishandling that obligation, which can rapidly degenerate into self-blaming.

Self-accuse prompts disgrace and with regards to self-blaming, that implies self-disgracing. Assuming on liability that isn't our own can incapacitate us, yet drag us down into the idleness of self-depreciation.

The way to self-acknowledgment and self-respect is perceiving that we are simply doing the best as we can and the way we are. We should accept the fact that flawlessness is blemished.

When a person goes to a point of self-acknowledgment that permits him/her to respect oneself with a greater sense of self-worth and high self-esteem. A person just needs to look at himself with a new perspective of self-worth if he intends to get away from this vicious circle of self-blaming.

A Narcissistic parent often pushes his child into this circle by excessive blaming and with unforgiving attitude towards the child's mistakes.

It's a well known fact that nobody is perfect. Some parent also induces this idea of perfection into the child by not appreciating the child enough which later creates many problems in upcoming stages of life. Everybody makes mistakes and everybody deserves a chance to learn from his/her mistakes; instead a narcissistic parent tries to make a lesson out of every mistake the child does, by excessive blaming and criticizing. Normally when a person does something wrong, instead of attempting to contribute to the inverse, a normal parent would make an open door for learning, contemplation, self-revelation and, at last, personal development, while a narcissistic parent does the opposite.

3.3 Need-Panic

Narcissistic father can easily turn his children into the individuals who are 'Need Panic' or in simpler words, they are the type of individuals who want somebody to be around them always so that they can work normally. Such children seek constant care and reassurance from their family, friends and other relationship, to do even the simplest of the tasks.

Such a father can easily turn the kids alarmed about their needs, who in turn find it baffling to deal with life situations alone and end up being very quiet about their needs or extremely baffled to deal with their problems on their own.

Sometimes, such kids might keep it up for a while and deal with the situation themselves, appearing to require nothing from their companions & friends. But as soon as something out of the way happens in their lives, they find themselves agitated and disturbed to their nails. Then panic and immediately turn to their so called friends and other relations for necessary help, not realizing that the biggest help would come from within themselves, after all.

Need panic children would perpetually look for

consistent consultation from others to decide the important decisions of their lives. The fastest way towards eliminating the need would be to serve the need immediately; which makes such individuals desperate and sooner than enough, they become the "needy" ones among their friends and colleagues.

3.4 Fierce Independence

Active and courageous children may react to narcissistic fathering by becoming 'fiercely-independent'.

They would desert and ultimately escape all emotional bonds that they might think would make them stick around other people. They develop firm believes by accepting that nobody can be trusted or depended on. They become the exact opposites of 'Need Panics" and can cause endless pain to themselves when they lose valuable people from their lives due to their non-trusting ability.

People will ultimately abandon them due to their extremely skeptical nature and the worst part is that they have already made up their mind about people losing them. This hurts them inside so they end up making bad choices and causing more harm to themselves. Sometimes, this becomes too painful for them, so, without much of a stretch, it can incite irregular 'Panic Need' occasionally.

Our minds are designed to live with other people in association. Having an understanding that we have individuals who we can go to when required causes us to feel sheltered and secure. Materials things are optional, regardless of whether significant. Having a relationship, you can depend upon causes us to behave normally and develop a normal healthy personality with fine traits.

Fierce independence is developed in a child when a parent is there for the child when there is a need for emotional support, so the child naturally feels relying on the parent for his/her emotional needs. This later develops into healthy habit of trusting other and depending on others in times of emotional needs. Such a child would grow up imagining that if and when he/she would need somebody, they will be there for him/her. This kind of connection later on in grown-up relations also implies that one is believing, ready to have maturity and security in a relationship without being frightful of the other individual leaving off, which can help grow very healthy and non problematic relationship.

However, a narcissistic parent would simply relinquish himself/herself from the emotional need of a child, causing the child feel deprived of emotional stability. Fiercely independent people often base their self-esteem and focus on their work, tend to build up very escaping or avoiding relationships where they don't trust their partner to be available for themselves in the times of need and also remove themselves in times when their partner might need them at emotional or critical times, in order to avoid dependence on partner or even letting the partner depend on them.

Such a person would also hate borrowing money from others or letting others do ordinary tasks for themselves. They would tend to not invite people unless they feel a strong need to do so. So often they are also taken as cold and harsh person who never really care about other people's feelings and people feel left out while in presence of such a person. Such a person can also be extremely stubborn when it comes to taking decisions of his/her life because they feel it's them who will have to endure everything alone in the end so why let the guards lose now when later they alone have to face the consequences of choices others are trying to make for them. So, they literally never let anyone take any kind of decisions for them or plan anything for them.

This leads to distorted and mistrusting relationships with a lot of emotional pain.

Then again, sensitive children may become passively selfless caretakers, who can only enjoy the feeling of being satisfied by providing undeserving and overly inflated, sometimes unwanted & unsought for, help to others. This way they tend to take back the caring and warmth that they have been missing all their lives. It might lead them to be exploited by some narcissistic partner, causing extreme emotional trauma and pain. Fierce independence is essentially an outcome of narcissistic upbringing of a child.

3.5 Insecurities about emotional attachment

Insecure attachment is the term given to a situation where insecurity arises when an individual's level of attachment increases with his/her partner.

This is caused by the abuse and deliberate caused by a narcissistic parent. The main reason behind this personality dysfunction is the repeated question in the mind of emotionally abused child that as to whether he/her would be safe when depending on others. Some people may ignore the voices in their brain and start trusting others, but in the end, they would always be worried about the 'degree of extent' to which they can (or should) trust people.

The disregarding emotional abuse caused by a narcissistic father, would end up making the child unable to deal with his/her own true feelings, resulting in the formation of multiple 'insecure attachments' with their friends and romantic partners.

Ultimately, such a relationship collapses and the child ends up being an individual who would 'avoid' any emotional attachment in order to safeguard his/her self from the pain caused by his/her own insecurities.

On the other hand, if an individual doesn't end up avoiding attachment, he/she takes up an opposite form, which is also a type of insecure attachment, called 'shaken panic inducing attachment'. This caused the person to be continuously restless and anxious about his/her partner, so he/she starts chasing and pursuing love bloodlessly, and once developing and attachment with somebody, becomes too clingy and irritated to deal with.

The association, the connection and sentiments we long for with our friends and family become a source of relentlessness for such a person, who finds losing everybody around him. Ultimately, escape and abandonment is the only way he/she might find to secure the inner hurt and pain which again cause some more pain and breach in someone character and reliability.

Regardless of whether you become on edge or avoidant relies upon an intricate blend of disposition and consistency in care and consideration, yet progressing disregard will in general make shirking, and eccentric consideration for the most.

3.6 Extreme Narcissism

Aggressive children, if handled wrongly by an abusive parent, would become extremely narcissistic in their lives, later. They would deal their own kids the same way they had been treated all their livers and even would add extra miseries in the lives of their children.

It's almost certain that they would certainly be emotional and physical abusers causing severe cases of 'domestic abuse'.

They would be the ones who would deliberately call themselves the smartest and the prettiest creatures on earth . They would bully others and get their joy from the pain caused to other people around them.

It is a fact that natural stubborn individuals with ranting disposition are the most sensitive inside who would turn up bad if faced with neglectful parenthood (fatherhood or motherhood or both).

It's like they're bound to wind up narcissistic themselves as they are like mirrors who reflect the exact image of whatever is thrown upon them. Extreme narcissists would always be eager to give their opinion to others in various matters, even when uncalled for. They develop a belief that they know everything and whatever they know stands correct irrespective of the ground facts. "They have a very hard time listening to others because they are often too busy thinking about their next lecture they want to deliver to others on their own believes. They consider themselves to be progressively significant, and increasingly powerful, then every other person. They tout their own achievements, overstates their significance, and needs to inspire other people's jealousy or enviousness. They accept that they are bound for incredible things.

Extreme narcissism slowly becomes an outrageous blend animosity, judgmental behavior and sadism. Extreme narcissistic person would constantly give out a threatening vibe to others. Such a person would regularly disrespect his own family and other friends and relationships in his life to the extent of dehumanizing the individuals with whom they are related.

3.7 PTSD *or* PNSD

"Post-Traumatic Stress Disorder" or essentially called PTSD is the consequence of unreasonably unforgiving narcissistic child rearing brought upon the youngster which can likewise be named as 'most noticeably awful character harm' of a kid.

If a person has a narcissistic parent or accomplice, they might have an idea that the narcissistic requires continuous praise and admiration from them. That might not be the most awful part —because narcissists need to control others, typically by isolating them from the ones who appreciate them. They're additionally continually attempting to bring down others' confidence.

Narcissistic parenting might include a wide range of incendiary and manipulative techniques, focused on bit by bit crushing the child's individuality. As narcissists need fearlessness and their confidence is low, they hurt a person in order to feel significant and make their life important.

Likewise, signs of narcissism change from individual to individual.

Narcissists may even not understand or mind how hurtful their conduct is, on the grounds that they are excessively bustling attempting to fulfill their own egotistical needs.

Tragically, narcissists' poisonous quality could be amazingly perilous and cause extreme mental harm to individuals who are normally presented to it. Subsequent to disposing of a narcissist, their exploited people ordinarily experience a time of vulnerability, misery, fierceness, or gloom, much like what happens following some trauma in the life of a normal individual. This condition is called Post Traumatic Stress Disorder (PNSD) or Post Narcissist Stress Disorder (PTSD).

Much like Post Traumatic Stress Disorder, PNSD is a condition that influences individuals who have been in close relationship with a narcissist. Living with a narcissist can be incredibly debilitating. Since narcissists are normally manipulative and damaging, the experience can scar a person forever. They attempt to gaslight their unfortunate victims by continuously blaming the wrongdoings of themselves on their victim.

Since narcissism isn't yet termed as a regular psychological abnormality in general, the exploited people have hardly any choices left to manage the circumstances.

The common reaction of PTSD or PNSD are bad memories flashbacks which may panic attacks and nervousness, shirking which leads to withdrawal from social experiences and extremely hurt and sensitive feelings. These symptoms express themselves in the form of elevated levels of frustration, outbursts of rage, a general hurtness about everything, sleepless nights, insomnia and a general inability to concentrate on basic regular assignments.

There's no doubt in the fact that a narcissistic parent would certainly damage the children in a way or other. PTSD is worst personality damage, which causes suicidal tendencies in children and a general fear for life. That can further prompt a dreadful way to deal with life. Emotional abuse generally tosses us into a condition of consistent alertness, taking everything happening in our lives as a risk and every effort served to evade the following risk. This prompts incessant anxiety and depression, with sudden flashback of abuse endured in the past, leading to emotional indifference and numbing and poor foresightedness about future. wherein individuals become so fixed on essentially enduring that they lose the capacity to envision life past the present. This causes real life problems later when dealing with grownup relationships.

3.8 Anxiety & Frustration

Constant worry and insecurities about yourself lead you to anxiety and depression as a result of Narcissistic patterning. Because a person loses the much needed integrity and emotional stability which is required to deal with problems and finding their solutions, resultantly, a person succumbs to sever anxiety and depression.

Depression is simply your brain's for overthinking for the repeated collision of logical reasoning and emotional logic. When your emotional world is a mess, logical reasoning can't find peace with emotional logic and so you enter into the world of Anxiety which is deep, dark abyss of unfruitful outcomes. There's a major distinction between what you do and what you do know. Regardless of whether you experience the ill effects of frenzy issue, summed up tension, or social fear, the way to hindering your psyche and body is figuring out how to endure dissatisfaction.

Severe depression and anxiety are the direct result of selfishness and cruelty brought upon by a narcissistic father.

Not only this, but you may also suffer from social phobia, panic disorders and extreme introvert disorder which will slowly turn your mind into a marshmallow which can't think anything good and you become a mess.

Anxiety and depression also cause frustration which can be defined by a person's inability to withstand stress and overcome obstacles. Narcissistic parent would try to shift a child's goal into his own selfish objectives, it leads to frustration and low tolerance in a child. That causes a general dissatisfaction in children leading them to develop many complexes.

Normal parent teaches their children about the hardships and difficulties that will be the part of life and how to deal with them while a narcissistic parent would start blaming the child for anything wrong done on his/her part. A normal parent won't try to arise stress in a child by repeating what wrong the child has done. By doing so, he/she allows the child to stabilizes his emotional energy if the child is feeling unhappy. Responding with dissatisfaction seemingly out of the blue, entangles numerous on edge people. Distinctions in disposition assume a job in adapting to unpleasant circumstances. A person with a low resistance for anxiety would show emotional impacts of pressure.

So as to feel less depressed by anxiety and frustration, you should accept the fact that problems are a necessary part of piece of life. Doing so permits you to relinquish the thought that something must not be right in case you're feeling troubled. Acknowledgment is realizing that sentiments are repeating, and once in a while the main path through is to brave the awkward feelings.

3.9 Social Anxiety Disorder (SAD)

Social anxiety disorder, commonly known as SAD or simply 'social phobia' is also a personality disorder which causes severe, overwhelming self-consciousness followed by anxiety and panic whenever a person is at a social gathering or in a regular everyday social confrontation. A person who suffers from 'social anxiety disorder' or 'Social Phobia' would feel an intense, persistent and chronic fear of being judged by other people around him. So, as a result, such person would feel embarrassed all the time and humiliated with his/her own actions.

A narcissistic parent would easily make the child insecure enough to feel paranoid about social situations that the child would develop a severe fear of facing other people which would eventually cause many problems at school and later at work and even in relationships of adult children. Such a child would be the target for bullying by other narcissistic people around him/her. This excessive and unreasonable fear of being around people often caused anxiety and depression in the end causing long-lasting dreads about certain situations and incidents in life. Such children would often worry-in-advance for things yet to happen. This leads to many personality complexes accompanied by low self-esteem.

Social Anxiety Disorder usually shows its symptoms when a person is around other people or they have to speak in front of other people. Once this phobia makes its roots strengthened in someone's personality, it's really hard to uproot it, leading to severe consequences, such as getting fired from job or getting excluded or even removed from a social gathering or friends group.

This personality disorder even caused abnormal physical symptoms in a person such as blushing, trembling, sweating, nauseated feelings, shaky voice and difficulty in speaking. The situation worsens when the above mentioned symptoms reciprocally increase the fear of rejection, becoming an additional layer of fear, causing the mind to perplex and react abnormally to a very normal situation, causing a vicious cycle of mental and emotional shocks to the person being affected.

A child brought up by a Narcissistic father would have a 100% more chance of developing this disorder as this disorder seems to get stronger when a person isn't allowed to speak his/her heart. A child with suppressed emotional growth would also suffer from this disorder more frequently. A Narcissistic parent would seldom allow the child to be himself/herself, resultantly an emotionally weaker and constantly worried child would develop social anxiety disorder while worrying about common and little things.

Once developed, this personality disorder also tends to run in families. It is often accompanied by anxiety and other frustration and depression related issues such as obsessive-compulsive disorder or Panic Attacks.

A Narcissistic parent can reinforce the idea on the child that he/she is not good enough or by simply comparing the child with other children who are more competent and brilliant. This can lead to the development of inferiority complex in the child which later piles up into truckload of insecurities, followed by 'Social anxiety disorder (SAN).

People with SAN tend to calm themselves in social situations with alcohol and drugs, and end up being the drug addicts and alcoholics.

***

UNDERSTANDING YOUR NARCISSTIC FATHER

4.1 Digging the roots of Father's Childhood

It's a fervently contested issue in the realm of psychiatry and no accurate reason for narcissistic character issue is known with an abundance of hypotheses about how does an individual become a narcissist? Similarly, as with character improvement and with other psychological wellness issue, the reason for narcissistic character issue is likely unpredictable. Narcissistic character issue might be connected to the following variables:

Environment: It may be due parent and youngster associations with either over the top veneration or unnecessary analysis that is inadequately sensitive to the kid's experience in light of the fact that a parent or caretaker couldn't give passionate consideration, or it could be the due to the reason; a parent gave an excessive amount of consideration and the kid never learned disappointment resistance.

Hereditary qualities: It may be due to an acquired attribute.

Neurobiology: It's an association between the brain and conduct and thinking. Narcissists accept they are extraordinary or unique and must be comprehended by other exceptional individuals. Additionally, they are unreasonably useful for anything normal or common. They just need to relate and be related with other high-status individuals, spots, and things. Other conceivable factor includes abnormalities in genes that influence the relation between the mind and conduct being over-sensitive.

Narcissistic individuals experienced significant distance, vacancy, weakness, and absence of importance. They came up short on the adequate inward structures to look after cohesiveness, strength, and a positive mental self-view to give a steady personality. Narcissists are unsure of the limits among themselves as well as other people and sway between separated conditions of self-swelling and mediocrity.

4.2 Understanding what Made Him Narcissistic

If you really want to cure your dad of his narcissism, then you might need to understand him better by digging around his past and the specific events happened in his life that actually made him such a person. Only then you would be able to provide a better healing aura and best of your help to your father who is in much of a need of treatment (right now).

Dig into your family tree, look for particular events that happened in your father's life and most importantly **look for the following signs in one of your paternal grandparents (or one of your paternal grandparents)** (which could have been the potential cause of inducing narcissism into your father's personality)

- **Living through your Father** – You need to check if your grandfather/grandmother were the type of people who always expected your father to follow them in every step they took. Did they forced your father to take up a career, or pick a college, or take some job that fulfilled the purpose of grandparents instead of the actual dreams of your father? Did they use to threaten your father with disownment if he refused to listen to them or disobeyed them?

- **Was your Father Marginalized by the Grandparents** – dig around if your grandparents were threatened by ability and potential success of your father. Did they encourage your father when he succeeded or did they tried to turn him down so that he may feel worse about himself whenever he succeeded at something? This might be the main cause your grandparents might have turned your father into a narcissist. of the child.

- **Manipulation** – Check if your grandparents were manipulative ones who always tried to guilt trap your father into doing whatever they wanted and desired. They never actually cared about your father and slowly turned him into the passive narcissist he has become today. Check if getting through things with your father, your grandfather always used blaming, shaming and emotional coercion as their tools to get him into doing whatever they desired him to do.

- **Superiority (Grandiosity)–** Did your grandparents always pressed an inflated sense of themselves which they always projected on your father, trying to prove that he was nothing and they were superior to them in every way.

- **No Empathy**–Dig around the roots of your father and check if he faced a childhood empty of much needed empathy a normal child must receive from his/her parents. It's a fact that this act on parent's parts would most likely turn the child into a narcissistic person.

- **Co-Dependency** – Did your grandparents always expected your father to take emotional, physical, and financial care of themselves? Did they expect him the same for the rest of his life? If so, there is a fair chance they might have pushed your father by guilt trapping him and by manipulating him. Look if your father tried to cut down the cycle of dependency and your grandparents responded with anger and utter selfishness of guilt shaming your father. If so, this might be the biggest reason they have pushed your father to be a narcissistic over the passage of time. Because a child will always try to follow the footsteps of his parents (no matte if he has himself become a parent), it's no shock that your father expects the same from you.

- **Self-centered and vain Grandparents-** Check if your grandparents were always self-centered who cared only about themselves with a higher sense of self-importance. They never gave importance to your father and his problems and always preferred their own problems (to deal with) rather than focusing on your father for a while or so. Also look if your grandparents were superficial who used to use other people for their benefit (used to exploit others).

- Did they used to take advantage of anybody who was in their circle? Also check if your grandparents only liked a surrounding where they were the center of attentions and they used to leave if they felt they aren't being given much of the importance they have been expecting. Were they charismatic persons who attracted everyone at the party or made others wish to be like them? Did they relish praise and admiration from everyone around them? Did they loved the spotlight and being the center of attention?

- Did they reinforce the alluring fantasies of their success, brilliance and prestige on your father all the times?

- Did they exaggerate their achievements and ambitions on your dad all the time?

- **Criticism rejecters-** Check if your grandparents were the ones who took criticism as something to help improve themselves. If not so, they might have subconsciously taught your dad the same thing and turned him into someone who feels strongly stung by criticism.

- Check if your grandparents used to cut people out of their lives who criticized them.

- **Rage problems**- Check if your grandparents had scary rage fits and they used to yell a lot at each other or at your father. Did they hurt each other or your dad with their anger? Also check if your grandparents were kind of people who were generally aloof and overall unsympathetic.

- Also check if your grandparents were around your father when he needed them the most. Also check if your grandparents dealt with your father in an indifferent way. Did they always want your dad to look good in front of their friends or accomplices? Did they bragged about your father when he did something good but ignored your dad completely when he failed at something?

If answer to most of the above mentioned signals from the two of your paternal grandparents or any one of your grandparents (or especially grandfather) is yes, then most probably your father went through a horrific childhood filled with so many emotional gaps that require and need emotional fulfilment and healing that can only be given to him by going back in time (that's why it's particularly difficult for a person with NPD to recover from this disorder because it might take a whole new life time for the person to understand somethings which hurt the person most at

that particular stage of his life.
***

CURING YOUR NARCISSTIC FATHER

The initial phase in getting help for your father towards curing from narcissism is acknowledging and accepting the fact there is a major issue with his conduct. Because it's a fact that a person can't recoup from something they won't recognize. So, the first step for you to cure your narcissist father also involves your recognition and acceptance that your father is suffering from Narcissistic Personality Disorder (NPD). Once you have recognized and accepted this fact, the next thing would be assuming certain positions in order to block the perpetual Narcissistic attacks on yourself. If you are with sound mind and emotional stability, only then you can help your father.

You might need to take the following steps in order to help your father dealing with NPD:

5.1 Resisting Narcissism

Narcissists are experts of the art, have idealized the strategy throughout the years, and through innumerable connections. They have contemplated You, reflected You, found your pleasure and torment focuses. In short they are specialists in what really matters to you. They are difficult to oppose in light of the fact that we are clung to them, and they will attempt each deceive in their arms stockpile to get back what they consider to have a place with them.

You might be a casualty of narcissistic maltreatment on the off chance that you have ever asked why you've been feeling increasingly on edge or discouraged in the past couple years. Likewise experiencing more difficulty dozing and feeling confounded or overpowered by conduct that you can't comprehend. For a child, it's a phase intended to exceed with the assistance of nice child rearing. Be that as it may, imagine a scenario where either of parents is narcissistic or in any case useless. Such families work as indicated by an implicit arrangement of rules. Youngsters comply with these principles, however never stop being tormented by them in light of the fact that the guidelines square passionate access to their folks ... and themselves. They become undetectable neither heard, seen, nor supported.

How might we recuperate from narcissistic maltreatment? What are antitoxins to such egotistical frenzy? In the first place, we have to have sympathy for us all managing narcissistic. Create self-acknowledgment and focus on relinquishing our own reckless propensities and complicity. Purposely practice sympathy and empathy. Abstain from focusing on the abuser or paying attention to him maybe this implies taking a news quick for some time so as to reconstruct an inner feeling of wellbeing. It's never past the point where it is possible to reclassify your feeling of self and focus on making new and better limits. Never let a narcissist decide your self-esteem.

5.2 Resisting Gaslighting attempts

The term gaslighting refers to when somebody controls you into addressing and re-thinking your world. What maybe individuals don't comprehend is the manner by which to oversee and adapt to it. It's normal that a narcissistic dad attempts to cause you to accept that you're whimsical or insane. He may disclose to you that you're not right when you're clearly right. He may guarantee you're recalling things wrong or causing things to up. When, as a general rule, that is what he's doing. He may communicate apparently earnest worry for your psychological prosperity; however, this is one of his stunts. It's a notable narcissistic control strategy. A most critical aspect regarding gaslighting is the denial of the real world. Being denied what you have seen. Being denied what you have encountered and know to be valid. It can cause you to feel like you are insane. In any case, you are not insane.

The individual who is gaslighting you will always be unable to see your perspective or assume liability for their activities. He will never get it. He will never say, yeah, you are right. Affirmation isn't on the cards. What's more, championing yourself isn't simply futile yet unsafe. Since the individual gaslighting will always be unable to react to rationale and reason, therefore, you must be the one to perceive that rationale and reason cannot be applied.

Perceive the example of undermining conduct.

Gaslighting possibly works when an individual doesn't know about what's happening. When you become alarm to the example, it won't influence you to such an extent. You might have the option to state to yourself, here we go once more and disregard it.

Remember that the Gaslighting isn't about you. It's about the gaslighter's requirement for control and force. Frequently the gaslighter is an extremely shaky individual. So as to feel equivalent, they have to feel unrivaled. So as to have a sense of security, they have to feel they have the high ground. They have scarcely any other adapting abilities or different approaches to arrange contrasts. That doesn't pardon the conduct. Yet, realizing that may assist you with thinking about it less literally while you conclude whether to keep up the relationship.

Know that you are probably not going to have the option to change the gaslighter in any event all alone. Gaslighting conduct is the main way gaslighters know to deal with their reality. Consequently, they are not liable to react to reasonable interests to change. It for the most part requires concentrated treatment, done eagerly, for a gaslighter to surrender it.

Reexamine whether the relationship merits enduring the consistent endeavors to work on your confidence. In the event that the gaslighter is your chief or administrator, begin searching for another activity. In the event that the individual is a relative or companion, think about how to put some separation between you. On the off chance that it's a huge other and you need to save the relationship, you will most likely need to demand couple's guiding.

Build up your own emotionally supportive network. You need others in your life who can affirm your world and worth. Gaslighters frequently attempt to disconnect their exploited people so as to remain in charge. They frequently further control their unfortunate casualties by over and over revealing to them that they are the main individual who truly cherishes and gets them. Try not to get it. Invest energy with loved ones. Look at your recognitions by conversing with others who saw what the gaslighter is raising doubt about.

Work on remaking your confidence. Advise yourself that you are a loveable and proficient individual, paying little mind to the assessment of the gaslighter. Assist yourself with recapturing point of view by helping yourself to remember different occasions throughout your life when you have felt grounded, normal, and for the most part great about yourself. It might be useful to keep a private diary in which you record occasions that the gaslighter is probably going to challenge. Record positive encounters and attestations of your own value also.

5.3 Setting Boundaries

A narcissistic dad will regularly cross your limits just to demonstrate that he can. He may appear excluded to your home or occasions. He may resist your family rules to show disdain toward you. He may deliberately give gifts just to the individual he likes, just to play mind games. You should define firm boundaries and authorize outcomes in the event that he goes too far. Clarify why you're laying down the law. This may feel like you're training a risky child. That is just how it is to deal with a naturally selfish dad.

Think before talking. Prior to visiting or addressing a narcissistic parent, you should consider that the parent is a narcissist. It may be useful to survey a portion of their glaring attributes so desires can be all the more suitably set.

Keep in mind, it is about him. It assists with having a desire that the discussion will turn towards the narcissist. While the underlying inquiry might be about the you, it rapidly changes to the narcissist. You ought to expect this and keep answers quick and painless to abstain from parting with an excessive amount of data. The narcissist will just utilize the extra information against you sometime in the future.

Decline to be cross examined. A run of the mill strategy of narcissists is to overpower others into a condition of increased uneasiness so they are less ready to think straight. When the narcissist starts, you should hinder their relaxing. At that point answer the inquiry they wish the narcissist posed rather than the one that was asked and quickly tail it with a commendation. This incapacitates and occupies most narcissists.

Reject verbal attacks. Another common narcissistic strategy is to obnoxiously ambush anybody they accept is a risk. you might get yourself an objective for a forceful, you are apathetic etc. remarks. This is about examination keeps up the narcissist's prevalent status. Be liberated from exploitation.

5.4 Getting professional and Medical Help for your Father

When your father is a Narcissist and you have confirmed the fact, then another fact also shows its face widely that you can't just leave your father for being narcissistic. Although, it's almost very very difficult to love him for his narcissistic nature when he almost makes you cringe with his selfish and cruel thoughts.

However, this is an issue related to your father's emotional wellness. Further, as your father ages, the narcissistic tendency might become less articulated and less disturbing as compared to what it used to be.

Regardless of whether your father is a mild narcissist, or an extreme one, it's a solid fact that your narcissist father is suffering from an emotional and psychological ailment and he needs your help.

It's a fact that there are no meds explicitly used to treat Narcissistic Personality Disorder yet. Treatment for Narcissistic Personality Disorder is discussion treatment which is likewise called psychotherapy. Meds might be remembered for treatment if father have other psychological well-being conditions.

Parents with narcissistic characteristics experience issues understanding and tolerating their children's sentiments. Research has discovered that individuals with narcissistic qualities experience issues dealing with their own feelings. They become restless, discouraged, or irate when they feel dismissed or even marginally reprimanded. Narcissistic parents need mindfulness and can't assume liability for how their conduct impacts their children.

However, if a parent is narcissist, it doesn't mean they have to remain as such. For example, when you figure out how to define limits with your narcissistic parent, after some time your stress will begin to reduce. This isn't a simple procedure! It takes practice, tolerance, and boldness. With the correct apparatuses, figuring out how to define limits with your narcissistic parent resembles building up other things in your life.

Psychotherapy can help your dad in the accompanying manner:

- Learn to relate better with you so your connections are increasingly private, agreeable and fulfilling.

- Understand the reasons for feelings and what drives to contend, to doubt others, and maybe to loathe yourself as well as other people.

- Accept and keep up genuine individual connections and coordinated effort with others.

- Increase capacity to comprehend and control sentiments.

- Understand and endure the effect of issues identified with your confidence

- Release your longing for unattainable objectives and perfect conditions and increase an acknowledgment of what's feasible and what you can achieve.

Treatment can be helpful during times of emergency, or can be given on a continuous premise to help accomplish and look after objectives. Frequently, including relatives or critical others in treatment can be useful. If you don't comprehend the circumstance, it can cause a ton of issues in your present connections. With the assistance of a professional, reliable advisor, you can start understanding these emotions and how to deal with them. You can work it out, recapture control, and feel good. Since communicating the issues can be extremely terrible, yet profoundly essential, addressing a fair-minded proficient helps a lot.

'Cognitive Behavioral Therapy (CBT)' is most commonly used talk therapy which is also termed as 'psychotherapy' which helps deal with mental and emotional disorders. CBT helps the patient uproot with their deeper wounds by making them better aware of negative thinking so they can view challenging and negative situations with a clearer view by enabling them to respond in a more positive way. CBT is a very helpful psychological tool which can be combined with other therapies when it comes to treating mental disorders, such as PTSD, depression, or other related disorders. Cognitive behavioral therapy CBT is also very effective in treating a wide range of problems in a quick way which results in better help with many specific challenges. CBT is helpful in treating all the following issues related to Narcissism:

- Manipulation
- Echoism
- Fierce Independence
- Superiority Complex
- Grandiosity and superficialness.
- Post-Traumatic Stress Disorder (PTSD)

- Extreme Narcissism
- Depression
- Phobias
- Anxiety disorders
- Sleep disorders & Eating Disorders
- Obsessive-compulsive disorder (OCD)
- Bipolar disorders
- Paranoia
- Schizophrenia

And other related disorders.

5.5 Providing Personal Help

It's a fact that it's very difficult to deal with a narcissist on personal level. Especially when the narcissist is your own father. He can be extremely stubborn, and yet very magnetic and convincing. Plus, you can't do much because you can't wave off this voice in your mind that he is my father and who he can behave like this with me.

The moment your father talks to you normally, with soft tone and bestowing some love, you feel your heart melting with the anticipation of some warm paternal affection.

But you must be strong. You mustn't ignore the fact that he is suffering from a certain 'mild mental illness'.

It's very important to keep in mind that if you didn't help your father with the cure, this might continue effecting every member of your family and while you are strong enough to understand and endure the damage with sane mind, others might not be strong on the same level and may go through insanity and other psychological problem which may affect their whole lives.

Look for the signs if your father is lying about things, or manipulating, disrespecting and treating others badly. Also look for the signs if he is giving enough space to everyone in the family to express themselves. Does he become excessively rude and even raging when somebody doesn't act according to his expectations?

Keep in mind that your father is suffering from NPD where he is totally unable to reciprocate the feelings of love and affection that you might be expecting from him. It's also not true that your father isn't willing to reciprocate the love and care; he simply isn't able to because he truly can't see you or hear you. He might even not be able to recognize you beyond his own bubble.

The most difficult thing might be your own self who becomes habitual of letting things inflict pain upon you. In such circumstances, your own personality becomes the biggest hurdle to take charge in its own hands because you have already lost a lot of confidence in yourself.

The first thing you need to do is to carefully consider your own goals and the positive changes you want to achieve while working on your goals.

What is the most influential thing that you have already worked upon with your father which actually worked in making him understand and care?

You also need to treat him softly with as much understanding as possible while treating him softly. You must avoid pointing out his hurtful words or dysfunctional attitude. You must never attempt to damage his image of perfection. Treat him as respectfully, calmly and gently as possible. Focus on how his behavior isn't the problem but the feeling that is imparted by his behavior. You must also remember to walk away when it becomes necessary (if the situation is ignited) to let things cool down. Then next thing is to implement the passive convincing with a gentle approach.

You must remember to not sent anything or define anything to a narcissistic individual if you yourself feel unwilling to keep for yourself.

However, when you have defined certain boundaries, there is a fair chance that he will rebel against the newly set boundaries. He might test your temperament, your limits, your extent of energy, so you should be well prepared mentally.

You must also be mentally prepared for any adverse, rebellious consequences.

Most important thing to remember is to never back down, or elsewise, you would be sending the fair signal that you're not to be taken seriously.

Your father can also feel threatened and insecure by the new changes you might be imparting on him as well as the surroundings and he can react adversely. Be prepared for that as well. To compensate what is being snatched from him, he might take some disturbing steps to punish you, or simply start manipulating you. At this stage, standing firm would be the only choice that would help both of you.

You must know that a person suffering from Narcissistic Personality Disorder would try to protect his insecurities and feelings of shame and inferiority, in order to make himself feel superior. You must keep in mind that your father is that particular person at this stage of his life and you are there to help.

You must accept the fact that he will try to deny his shortcomings and mistakes. He will also try to project his faults on you or other family members. You might feel yourself going into a whole new phase of depression and anxiety with all of this coming down on you because it's a fact that a normal person finds it utterly upsetting to get directly blamed for things. You must always remember that you don't have to take any of this personal.

Keep in mind that your narcissistic father isn't living in the reality; rather he has this own world of dark imaginations where everything and everybody has a predesigned space and place which can't be altered so easily. No matter what you do, he won't buy your views. You must also remember to protect yourself from becoming a narcissist yourself.

Another important thing is to not argue with your father suffering from NPD. He might look a completely healthy, normal and sane person but he isn't a normal person. He has a personality disorder which requires cure and healing. Moreover, arguing will only ignite the already burning fire more which can adversely affect the situation against the positive expectations.

There would come a point when you will also have to let go of your desire and need for approval. Simply detach yourself from his expectation to get pleased on the expense of your (or other family member's) happiness. Even if he would want to sees the things differently, you need to stand firm and have trust that things are going to be change positively and that positivity is brought upon by you. (take that as a blessing while keeping yourself blissful for more upcoming blessings)

In the meanwhile, while you are dealing with all the negative energy and stress, you must look for much needed support for yourself from someone else who supports you in your life. This will help you to erase the negativity caused by narcissistic tendencies.

The best barrier against the abuse and projections of the narcissist is a solid feeling of self. At the point when you know your own qualities and shortcomings, it's simpler to dismiss any out of line reactions leveled against you.

You are also well aware of the fact that you are going to live with your father and you will have to endure him. Now when you are going to remain in an association with a father suffering from NPD, you need to be straightforward with yourself about what you can (or can't) anticipate. It's also a fact that your narcissistic father won't change into somebody who really values you, so you'll have to search somewhere else for fulfilling the gap. It might be your mother, your sibling or some other fatherly figure.

You also need to realize that you also originate from a narcissistic family, you might also not have a good feeling of what a solid give-and-take relationship is.

In the meanwhile, don't forget to invest your own energy with people who really love you for what you are. Such people in your life will give you a legitimate feeling about love and your true self with boasted confidence and self-esteem. So as to keep up point of view and abstain from becoming tied up with the narcissist's contortions, it's essential to invest energy with individuals who know you as you truly are and approve your considerations and sentiments.

Also don't forget to make new friends to keep yourself outside the narcissistic circle for a while when you boost up your positive energies. , It might be a good possibility that your father has isolated you from other people in order to have a better control over your life (as well as other family members). In such a situation, you must manage to get outside that influence, build your confidence and seek for healthy and positive relationships. You might also need extra time to rebuild lapsed relationships and friendships and creating new healthy relationships.

Looking for some purpose in your work and investing your time into something creative would also help keeping yourself positive and well away from the bad influences of narcissistic practices. Also keep pursuing such activities that might highlight your talents.

Enduring a narcissistic relationship is always very difficult especially when it's your father. It's very easy trap to become distracted while dealing with a narcissistic patient. Feeling "gaslighted" by the manipulation caused by your father would make you feel overwhelmed.

In case you are living in codependency with your father, you may need to preserve to the sense of self.

Keep firm believe that you don't deserve to be treated like this, you don't deserve to be bullied emotionally by your own father. It's unfair and uncalled for.

Next thing you need is to educate yourself as much about narcissism and 'Narcissistic Personality Disorder (NPD)'. Educating yourself about NPD will make you recognize and learn about all the tactics and behavioral patterns shared by a narcissist.

This will help you cope with curing your narcissistic father.

Confronting a narcissist is another bigger problem which you'll have to deal after the balloon of his fake ego has burst up.

FORGIVING YOUR FATHER

Once you've figured out that one or more of your parents are narcissists, suffering from Narcissistic Personality Disorder (NPD), now it's time to understand that your father is suffering from an illness which may be a result of many deep rooted problems along with narcissism continuum. Whatever the reality is or however dark the circumstances become, you need to move forward with your own life. And moving forward won't start unless you start forgiving the person who has been cause of all your emotional pain and depravity.

Following are some of the ways by which you would help yourself with this forgiving routine and at the same time help yourself with some ground rules to avoid further future pain.

6.1 Asserting Boundaries Resisting Narcissism

A normal person inclines toward an answer that is commonly pleasing. That is not how a narcissistic personality functions. A narcissistic father might only flourish with the feeling of control. This is abnormal and unhealthy behavior which is not acceptable by a normal person. It's quite natural that your dad may esteem his capacity to control you on having a normal, healthy romantic relationship. At that point, you won't find your dad to bargain or yield on issues. It is at that point when your narcissistic dad will cross the boundaries to your personal and individual freedom. He may challenge your family rules to show disdain toward you. He may purposefully give presents and gifts only to those people around you whom he likes. You should define firm boundaries limits and authorize consequences if your boundaries are disrespected and crossed (Although give him a fair chance to earn respect for your boundaries) and he goes too far. Clarify why you're laying down the law.

This may feel weird and even disrespectful towards your dad but you should keep in mind that you are doing this for something good.

Narcissists continually disregard limits. They see others, especially their youngsters, as augmentations of themselves to control and control. So, it's your main responsibility is to reflect what the narcissist wishes to find in himself and wishes to show to the world. As the substitute, your main responsibility is to assume the fault for the family's issues, persevere through the narcissist's most exceedingly awful maltreatment, and handle irrational obligations. In any case, as the narcissist's child, you are externalized, not regarded as an individual with your own character. Your own father is the one who considers your demands and ideas as crazy, bogus, or unsafe. One of the most troublesome and significant things you should accomplish for yourself as a survivor is to set up proper boundaries. It's also very important as this might be the only thing that would help you to get through a lot of things during all those stress and depression. Understanding what that implies and getting happy with doing it can require some investment and practice for the offspring of a narcissist. The primary spot to begin is with the narcissist parent and potentially other relatives. It's also a very strong fact that the vast majority of us love our parents, regardless of what sick emotional and personality damage they put us through. We stick to our requirement for adoration and approval from them. Your narcissistic parent can't cherish you genuinely the manner in which we as a whole have the right to be adored inside our families, and so far as that is concerned is able to do close to short lived sympathy. However, you may in any case love that parent. Blended in with sadness and outrage, you may likewise feel for your parent's NPD. It is additionally conceivable that you are numb to your parent or too utilized something like feel love any longer.

However just remember that the most helpful thing in the whole process would be your sincere effort to not pass any judgement or be harsh with yourself for any of it.

Make an effort to respect your own emotions. Let your emotions guide you to take decisions which root in your true deeper self and which help you to connect to your father and other family members. You may also quit responding to your family for a while if that is the most important thing for you to heel at that time. After a while you may start working with them again after setting some ground rules for your boundaries and how they should respect those boundaries (especially your narcissistic father).

Go no contact if that feels like the most secure decision. Narcissist fathers except if they are genuine savages, are generally fit and safe for friendship for their children. Some might have the option to give in manners that you find supporting or accommodating.

6.2 Recognize your Role in Family

Is it safe to say that you were a substitute or the prodigy? Have you acted now and again as a flying monkey? Jobs are regularly liquid in the narcissistic family, contingent upon the narcissist's plan. Maybe you have been the prodigy and furthermore scapegoated. Since the narcissist keeps up control by making divisions (separate and vanquish) among relatives, you may feel distanced from your other parent and kin. Maybe you feel deceived by them. Remember that every one of you have been a piece of a twisted framework arranged by the predominant narcissist in the family uniquely to serve his needs to the detriment of others. In some way or another you have all been battling to get by with the jobs you have been thrown in.

Sometimes, it's difficult to turn to entirely new setup with a new set of emotions and entirely new practices, particularly ones that cause us to feel abnormal. It reveals to us change is excessively hard. Sometimes things might not work the way they are supposed to work, however, with positivity, eventually you will find the ability to manage any hardships coming your way.

6.3 Educate yourself about Narcissism

As a matter of first importance, there is nothing of the sort as a narcissist who does not know they are a narcissist. What's more, as The Thing let me know, they do everything deliberately. Narcissists have no ethical focus or character of their own. They influence our compassion and passionate insight to get what they need. They likewise dislike the reaction out of us for the force it gives us, when we're onto them. Narcissists don't encounter discrete feelings. They don't feel misery, blame, satisfaction... all they experience is the increase in fuel that our feelings particularly perplexity, bewilderment, disappointment and outrage give them.

Individuals with Narcissistic Adaptations regularly take a stab at turning into "the best" in their field on the grounds that noticeable achievement and status matter more to them than they do to most others. Numerous Narcissists are urged to exceed expectations at work by their folks, however are not shown the essential abilities to exceed expectations at closeness. This makes it likely that they will look for some kind of employment more satisfying than family life and, in this way, dedicate more vitality to it. Somebody who is glad to invest their free energy with their accomplice and kids is bound to spend less hours at work. Once you can perceive the example of individual qualities, shortages, and adapting aptitudes that we call Narcissistic Personality Disorder, you are probably going to be shocked at exactly what number of individuals you have in your life that fit that depiction.

6.3 Forgive your Father

The past can't be changed, just comprehended. At the point when forgiveness is certifiable, it has an incredible transformational impact. Keep in mind, pardoning is for the forgiver, not the guilty party. It is smarter to genuinely excuse in little lumps one after another, as opposed to conceding cover pardoning. This permits space for other future or past offenses to be acknowledged and worked through altogether. Try not to constrain this progression, do it an agreeable pace so the advantages will be life enduring.

A part of forgiving your father also means that your Narcissist father won't Change as you want him to change because for that to happen he might have to go back in time to do the same what you have been doing right now (trying to understand your narcissistic father and remaining a normal sane person with healthy mind and perfect personality)

This might feel the most difficult challenge at time and rather tiresome when you are trying to put a lot of effort through something, knowing that it won't be as fruitful as your high expectations, still you have to remain positive about the fact that even a small change towards positivity is a very big positive breakthrough which will change things for your father in a great deal positively when it comes to his personality restoration.

You should also keep in mind that the likelihood of change in your narcissistic father is one in a thousand. Still you can't stop believing in good things and all the good things your father can be. Above all, it depends a great deal on your father's motivation and acceptance towards change which depends on his understanding that he is suffering from some disorder. It's a psychological fact that changing oneself after 30s is somewhat challenging task because of the firm believes and behavioral patterns a person has adopted after all these years.

Now if your father decides to make efforts towards a healthier mindset and a greater personal self then there is literally nothing better than this. But even if he does so, you might be better to assume no positive outcome (this will help you to not get your expectations too high hence avoiding you frustration in the end). Because nobody can deny the fact about the great unchangeable nature of a Narcissists

They seldom (truly)change.

Even if sometimes they act nicely it might be another manipulative maneuver. Keep your hopes high though, because your main focus is to heal yourself and forget every abusive emotion you have experienced and ultimately forgive your father so that you are free from the pain you have been holding for so long. You are dropping off that burden that has held you down for so long. You are freeing yourself from the aching that wounds your heart.

Remember at whatever stage you are at your right now or whatever reality you are facing down right now at your life, you can't deny the solid fact that you can't stay still and you always need to move forward for a normal healthy life.

It's never too late to heal from something that

causes you pain of any sort. It's your time to heal and move past your pain.

You are the decision maker of your own life.

Also remember that it's never too late to set boundaries for your own good. Similarly, it's never too early to set limits as well for a greater personal self

It's your right to work on your own healing.

It doesn't matter even if you don't have any job and still living a dependent life. You can always help yourself.

CURING YOURSELF FROM THE DAMAGE

7.1 Attune with your Feelings

As the offspring of a narcissist parent, you have been methodically prepared to overlook your sentiments, even to dread and loathe them. Your emotions are an immediate risk to the narcissist parent since they are probably going to strife with what she needs, accepts, and requests. In the narcissistic family, just the narcissist's emotions matter, and every other person's must be sublimated or inside and out squashed through scorn, disgrace, rage, and different types of assault.

Maybe the most significant activity for yourself toward mending is to reconnect with your sentiments. They are there, and they generally have been. Give them access, hear them out, convey them with deference. In your emotions you will find yourself and your way through and out of the narcissist's "elective realities" world. Since you have been disregarded in countless manners by your parent(s), you should explore through serious hurt and outrage. Most narcissists continually venture their own bankrupt intentions and feelings onto others and censure others for or even blame them for their own oppressive conduct, so from the start you may not realize what you truly feel versus what you have been mentally programmed to accept. As you figure out how to adjust to your sentiments, show restraint. Make an effort not to pass judgment on yourself.

7.2 Don't blame yourself

Particularly in the event that you've been abused by your family, you are probably going to naturally accuse yourself and feel blame for things outside your ability to control or duty. Narcissists are specialists at diverting and anticipating fault onto others. On the off chance that they seethed at you and you went to bat for yourself, you assaulted them. On the off chance that they punched you, you drove them to it. Perhaps the most ideal approaches to break your unfortunate relational peculiarities is to quit reprimanding yourself for what was never your duty or shortcoming in the first place.

7.3 Stop Hurting Yourself

Alongside not accusing yourself, chances are you have to stop examples of self-misuse. As somebody brought up in a narcissistic family, you are inclined to unsafe, self-rebuffing, and self-calming yet damaging practices, for example, substance misuse and addictions, self-mischief, and rush chasing. Your reckless conduct is a disguise of the narcissistic maltreatment you grew up with, which is something contrary to the narcissist's externalization of torment. By taking part in such conduct you keep on giving the narcissist control over you. You likewise fuel the enthusiastic and physiological injury you have just persevered. Examples of dependence and self-mischief can be very difficult to break, so look for help and backing from individuals who comprehend the elements of narcissism.

7.4 Give yourself the depleted Respect

The vast majority of us love our folks, regardless, and we stick to our requirement for adoration and approval from them. Your narcissistic parent can't adore you unequivocally the manner in which we as a whole have the right to be cherished inside our families, and so far as that is concerned is able to do close to momentary sympathy. However, you may in any case love that parent. Blended in with despondency and outrage, you may likewise feel for your parent's NPD. It is likewise conceivable that you are numb to your parent or too utilized around feel love any longer.

Whatever you feel, make an effort not to pass judgment on yourself for it. Respect your emotions and let them be your guide by the way you decide to associate with your family. Go no contact if that feels like the most secure decision. Or then again work with firm limits and brought down desires. Narcissist guardians, except if they are genuine perverted people, are typically equipped for friendship for their youngsters, at any rate once in a while. Some might have the option to give in manners that you find supporting or accommodating. With a sound portion of suspicion, take the great when it comes, as constrained as it might be.

It's also a fact that kids who are raised by a narcissist father are most likely to pick up at least some narcissistic traits during their life time. You might call them narcissist bugs which sneak into your personality to create little bit of disturbances in letting yourself be a totally normally person even if they don't infest you fully. Sometimes, they may overcome and turn you into an extreme narcissist; however, with the help of your own self, you can overcome the bad effects of narcissist bugs from your personality. Some healthy behavioral patterns and mindfulness also helps to get rid of these bugs.

Investigate yourself. What do you do that helps you to remember your narcissist mother or father? Do you look for consideration or control through blame or control? Would you be able to be increasingly delicate to other's emotions and points of view?

The best retribution is a well-lived healthy life. Work on care and harmony in your own life. You can't help how you were raised, however you can work to control how you act now and how you bring up your own little angels.

This most difficult stage of all of this might be progressively troublesome as the effect of the narcissism is figured it out. Then counts the time which you might have spent dealing with narcissistic effects; the additional time that is spent doing the progression, the more prominent the effect of the recuperating.

Remember both positive and negative things which came about out of the narcissism.

While moving ahead, you will also observe that some oppressive conduct with respect to the narcissistic parent got clear. Mistreatment for a child could be physical (restriction, animosity), mental (gaslighting, Silent-treatment), verbal (criticism), blaming, financial (neglect, inordinate gifting), and sexual (embarrassment).

Release your anger if it's the most important requirement you feel at the moment. Outrage and anger is a normal reaction after the dabs have been associated and the misuse (abuse) has been recognized. It is difficult to accept that a parent who ought to be cherishing and kind would do the things they have done. Whatever picture an individual had of their narcissistic parent is presently totally broken. It's a natural fact that some sort of rage and anger could be anticipated on your mother too for not shielding you from your narcissistic father.

Sometimes the annoyance is disguised for not understanding or facing sooner. It is critical to release the agony and pain in a sound way, for example, crying in front of some close emotional relationship.

If you feel this way to step back for some time to increase a superior point of view, then do so by all means. Start by thinking about how the narcissistic parent's contorted picture of the world and individuals molded your current thoughts, sentiments and convictions. Neutralize the twisted pictures, with a now enhanced and better picture of the real world around you. This basic advance liberates an individual from the narcissistic lies and fake beliefs.

Remember, your past has already been written

with and un-erasable ink. It can't be changed now. The only help it can provide is better understanding of present and thus a better help for future.

Forgiving, at one stage becomes inevitable, for it holds an incredible transformational impact. Just remember that in forgiveness there lies your own redemption first before it could be granted to the abuser. For absolution is for the forgiver, not the wrongdoer. It is also helpful to forgive bit by bit rather than forgiving at once; slowly releasing your burden would last forever then taking it off all at once and then after a while reloading it over your head.

This also permits space for other future or past offenses to be acknowledged and worked through in a careful way.

When there's a narcissistic character in your circle, you can detect them instantly by the fact that they would be drawing a lot of attention and the general admiration would seem to be drawn to their direction. That is by structure — regardless of whether it's pessimistic or constructive consideration, those with narcissistic characters make a solid effort to keep themselves in the spotlight.

You may before long end up becoming tied up with this strategy, pushing aside your own needs to keep them fulfilled.

In case you're sitting tight for a break in their consideration looking for conduct, it might never come. Regardless of the amount you modify your life to suit to their needs, it's never going to be sufficient.

On the off chance that you should manage a narcissistic character, don't permit them to invade your feeling of self or characterize your reality. You matter, as well. Routinely help yourself to remember your qualities, wants, and objectives.

Assume responsibility and cut out a bit of "personal time." Take care of yourself first and recall that it's not your business to fix them.

There are times when disregarding something or basically leaving is a suitable reaction.

Similarly, it also depends on the type of relationship you are dealing with, for example, now that you have a basic understanding of what narcissism is, you might also be able to detect some narcissistic traits in your boss, your sibling, one of your friends, or even a neighbor. At that point you have to decide what type of behavior you need to adopt with them. This book is particularly dealing with narcissistic father issues, so in real life you might have to adopt a bit different strategies when it comes to other narcissistic relationships you are dealing with. Similarly, their effect on you also depends on the deepness of emotional attachment with each person.

So, it's a clear fact that a great of your response relies upon the type of relationship.

A few people with narcissistic characters appreciate making others squirm. On the off chance that that is the situation, do whatever it takes not to get obviously bothered or show inconvenience, as that will just urge them to proceed.

In the event that it's somebody you'd prefer to keep close in your life, at that point you deserve to make some noise. Attempt to do this in a quiet, delicate way.

You should reveal to them how their words and lead sway your life. Be explicit and steady about what's not satisfactory and how you hope to be dealt with. In any case, set yourself up for the way that they may just not comprehend — or care.

When taking all the above mentioned steps on the road to cure yourself from the toxic impacts of a narcissistic father, you will feel yourself much stronger and much better able to distinguish different narcissists at work or in other social networks. This recognition will help you to protect yourself from all their harmful effects when you will never again allow them or their useless conduct to cause or produce moments of depression and anxiety to yourself. Getting yourself well aware about narcissism will automatically disarm a narcissistic as he/she would be totally incapacitated in light of the fact that there could never again cause a scary impact on you.

7.5 GROW

Remember, it's important to give yourself enough time to grieve over the pain you have been enduring all these years. No matter how much positivity you try to keep within yourself, you will end up feeling aloof, angry, sad, confused, low at confidence, broken and grieving most of the time. The flashbacks of bad memories will keep you down whenever you try to hit life at a point higher than before.

Don't lose hope and use the pain to help you 'GROW'.

Find the best support from your family and friends

and let yourself 'heal'.

Give yourself time, spoil yourself for a while, do anything necessary to bring you back on the track of right mindedness with all bad memories erased or at least faded away. At times you might regret at the loss of your childhood dreams and goals.

You must also accept the fact that healing takes time. Even a small splinter pains the body and healing from the smallest wounds of splinter takes time; it's also a wound on your soul that was inflicted by a narcissistic father upon your whole life as you may have lived. Think of it as a wound; but now the only difference is that you have taken care of the wound and it's in the process of recovery.

You have already taken care of so many things by yourself. You are stronger and higher than the pain.

It can't fail you. You are the one who will fail this pain. You are the one who will win over. Just have firm faith in yourself. While you are healing, you might not expect your father to understand your pain and the healing process as he might be fighting another whole different of fight with himself while recovering from the dysfunction.

If you have yourself developed NPD, you might find yourself very reluctant to even admit this fact that you are suffering from Narcissistic Personality Disorder. Even if you admit this to yourself, you might find yourself extremely reluctant share the fact with anybody and seek help. Narcissistic Personality Disorder is just like some bad addiction. Getting on to this addiction is easy, while letting go is as hard as it can be.

However, this very fact does no way mean that there's no positive hope. First thing is your willingness to accept change and do efforts to bring on the positive change.

Getting on board with a skilled therapist can help a lot in making you learn to take the responsibility and grow.

CONCLUSION

Living with somebody who has Narcissistic Personality Disorder (NPD) is somewhat similar to living in another reality where you are relied upon to acknowledge whatever that individual says or does, even if it's clearly wrong and off-base. It's as difficult as life can be because there is no other way to oblige a narcissist or to abandon them to dwell on their own (which is sometimes very difficult and painful because they are your loved ones). If you stay and object, you are made to feel as if it was all your fault.

Even if you are trying your best and dealing with everything that may come along with, sooner or later you would start to get excessively drained or terrified of the entire situation and the circumstances brought upon you by a person suffering from NPD.

It is sometimes very difficult to deal with a narcissistic parent; however, after understanding yourself the roots and causes of narcissism, you can provide the much needed help to paint the bigger picture of your life beautiful.